W9-BPJ-484

What's Your X-FILES I.Q.?

Over 1,000 Questions and Answers for Fans

MARC SHAPIRO

A CITADEL PRESS BOOK
Published by Carol Publishing Group

A Citadel Press Book
Published by Carol Publishing Group
Citadel Press is a registered trademark of Carol Communications, Inc.

Editorial, sales and distribution, and rights and permissions inquiries should be addressed to Carol Publishing Group, 120 Enterprise Avenue, Secaucus, N.J. 07094.

In Canada: Canadian Manda Group, One Atlantic Avenue, Suite 105, Toronto, Ontario M6K 3E7

Carol Publishing Group books may be purchased in bulk at special discounts for sales promotion, fund-raising, or educational purposes. Special editions can be created to specifications. For details, contact Special Sales Department, Carol Publishing Group, 120 Enterprise Avenue, Secaucus, N.J. 07094.

Manufactured in the United States of America
10 9 8 7 6 5 4 3 2 1

Library of Congress Cataloging-in-Publication Data

Shapiro, Marc.
    What's your "X-files" I.Q.? : Over 1,000 questions and answers for fans / Marc Shapiro.
        p.   cm.
    "A Citadel Press book."
    ISBN 0-8065-1927-4 (pb)
    1. X-files (Television program)—Miscellanea.   I. Title.
PN1992.77.X22S52   1997
791.45'72—dc21   97-26973
                                                              CIP

What's Your
X-FILES
I.Q.?

Gillian Anderson and David Duchovny. © 1997 Fox Broadcasting Company. Photo credit: Michael Lavine/FOX.

CONTENTS

ACKNOWLEDGMENTS

I would like to thank my loving wife Nancy who kept reminding me to tape season four episodes; my loving daughter Rachael who has had it up to here with any sentence containing the words X-Files; Bennie and Freda: you know why; my agent Lori Perkins who is doing her damnedest to make sure all my bills get paid; Lisa Kaufman at Carol Publishing Group for her enthusiasm; Charles Bukowski, Patti Smith, Black Sabbath, and Kiss for being there in a very X-Files sort of way; the countless websites and printed sources bound and determined to make trivia an essential and maddening element of *The X-Files* phenomenon; and finally, everybody connected to *The X-Files*, for being just too damned hip for this planet.

INTRODUCTION

More than a thousand *X-Files* websites worldwide can't be wrong! *The X-Files* is the Holy Grail when it comes to bizarre details, little-known facts, and obscure, bordering-on-downright-anal, references.

The X-Files, which debuted September 10, 1993, has proved a delightfully wicked journey to the dark side of paranormal incidents, mutants and monsters, government conspiracies and coverups, and alien secrets. True-believer FBI Agent Fox Mulder and his skeptical partner Dana Scully—and a shadowy cast of supporting characters like The Lone Gunmen, Deep Throat, Mr. X, and Cigarette Smoking Man—have made the unreal tantalizingly real for millions of viewers and the catchphrase "Trust No One" a rallying cry for a constantly growing cadre of hip, savvy, and intelligent *X-Files* fanatics.

What's Your X-Files I.Q.? is the ultimate test of your knowledge of the *X-Files* experience. And since more and more *X* fans have been discovering the show each season, the book is designed to be friendly to those who got on the bus late.

Kick off your *X-Files* test with a maddening array of true/false, multiple choice, and question-and-answer brain-teasers, with a season-by-season, episode-by-episode break-down that includes the recently wrapped season four. Jump in at any time. Then test your knowledge of the facts behind Agents Mulder and Scully and their real-life alter egos David Duchovny and Gillian Anderson.

If you're still standing, wade through the pages of general *X-Files* obscura guaranteed to drive you up the wall.

Let's keep scoring simple. One point for a right answer. No points for a wrong answer. Don't worry about tie breakers. There won't be a need for one.

Welcome to the world of *X-Files* trivia. The Truth Is Out There . . . somewhere.

What's Your
X-FILES
I.Q.?

Mulder and Scully investigate the work of Manitou, a man that
can change shapes and become an animal. © 1994 Fox
Broadcasting Company/Photo Credit: Ken Staniforth/FOX.

1

SEASON ONE

"The X-Files"

1 What were the words that flashed across the TV screen before the pilot episode began?

2 What were the first words Mulder said to Scully?

3 What was the name and occupation of Scully's lover in an early draft of the script? (He was eliminated before the episode was shot.)

4 Mulder is seen eating his favorite snack food for the first time. What is it?
    A. Sunflower seeds
    B. Peanuts
    C. Cheese wedges

5 TRUE OR FALSE: The only visible cause of Karen Swenson's death was a nosebleed and two small pink lumps on her lower back.

6 What did Mulder spray-paint on the road after hearing strange noises and why?

7 How does Scully describe the lost time?
    A. A time slip
    B. A warp continuum fracture
    C. A universal invariant

"Deep Throat"

8 Anita Budahas is accused of what crime?

9 Where does Mulder meet Deep Throat for the first time?
   A. In the lobby of the Watergate Hotel
   B. In the restroom of a Washington bar
   C. In the hallway outside Scully's apartment

10 TRUE OR FALSE: The restaurant where UFO buffs gather is called The Flying Saucer Restaurant.

11 What is Paul Mossinger's occupation?

12 What is the name of the area where UFO parts are allegedly stored?

13 What is the code name for the man tailing Mulder and Scully?
   A. Redbird
   B. Jefferson
   C. Cigarette Smoking Man

14 What does Mulder discover about Ellens Air Force Base?

15 Scully discovers the identity of Redbird. Who is he?

16 Where does Mulder meet Deep Throat at the end of the episode?

"Squeeze"

17 How does George Usher's killer escape?
   A. Through the razor blade discard slot in the medicine cabinet
   B. Through a six-by-eighteen inch air vent
   C. Under a crack in the hotel room door

18 How was Usher killed?

19 Where does Scully's old Academy classmate work?

20 In which city have the serial killings taken place?
   A. Baltimore
   B. Los Angeles
   C. Vancouver

21 Mulder discovers that the murder is similar to an X-File dating back to what year?

22 What does Eugene Tooms, a suspect in the killing, do what for a living?

23 What is Tooms's address?

24 What is Tooms's room number?

25 Where is Tooms finally captured?

26 What do genetic tests on Tooms disclose?

"Conduit"

27 Mulder does what for the first time in the episode "Conduit"?
   A. Prays
   B. Has a drink
   C. Eats sunflower seeds

28 Where was Ruby Morris when she vanished?

29 What information is in the file Blevins shows Scully?
   A. The truth about Mulder's parents
   B. Information about the abduction of Mulder's sister Samantha
   C. New information on Tooms

30 Darlene Morris's 1967 UFO sighting is on file with what organization?

31 TRUE OR FALSE: Kevin Morris's drawings consist of weirdly shaped zeros and ones.

32 What is the name of the biker bar where Greg worked?
  A. The Biker Bar
  B. The Pennsylvania Pub
  C. Backwoods Lounge

33 What is the name of the government goon who threatens Mulder?

34 What do Mulder and Scully discover about Kevin's drawings?

35 What does Mulder discover when he returns to Ruby's abduction site?

36 What leads Mulder to Greg Randell's body?

37 Who says "The truth has brought me nothing but heartache."

38 Ruby is finally found and is showing signs of what ailment?
  A. Malnutrition
  B. Prolonged weightlessness
  C. Blood loss

"The Jersey Devil"

39 What year does the first attack by the creature take place?

40 Mulder is doing "research" on the case by reading what kind of magazine?

41 Which body parts is the recent victim of the creature missing?
  A. An arm and a leg
  B. Two legs
  C. The head and an arm

42 What is the name of the most recent victim?

43 Scully meets Rob, the attractive divorced dad, at what function?

44 How is the female creature killed?

45 What does the autopsy on the female creature indicate?

46 Rob invites Scully on another date. Where does he plan on taking her?

47 She turns him down, preferring to do what instead?
  A. Go back to Mulder's apartment to write up the report
  B. Go home alone
  C. Accompany Mulder to the Smithsonian Institute to report his findings

"Shadows"

48 What is HTG Industrial Technologies?

49 What is the first indication of a ghostly presence in Howard Graves's office?

50 What was unusual about the bodies taken to Bethesda Naval Hospital?

51 How does Mulder secretly get the corpses' thumbprints?
  A. He presses the thumbs against a glass.
  B. He presses the thumbs against the lenses of his glasses.

C. He presses the thumbs against the polished surface of his belt buckle.

52 What is the name of Howard Graves's successor?

53 What happens when Dorlund grabs Lauren Kyte?

54 Name one of the dead terrorists and his terrorist group.

55 TRUE OR FALSE: When Mulder and Scully get in their car, a sharp static charge leaps out of the radio, knocking them back against the seat.

56 What does Lauren find in her apartment after hearing muffled, anguished voices?

57 How does the FBI discover the evidence of the illegal operation?

"Ghost in the Machine"

58 How is Eurisko CEO Benjamin Drake killed?

59 Agent Jerry Lamana previously worked with Mulder in what FBI division?

60 While in the Eurisko complex, Mulder and Scully's elevator stops above which floor?

61 Who steals Mulder's killer profile notes?
A. Brad Wilczek
B. Deep Throat
C. Jerry Lamana

62 What happens after Scully goes to bed?

63 How does Lamana die?

64 Deep Throat informs Mulder that Wilczek has invented what kind of computer?

65 TRUE OR FALSE: Scully and Mulder gain access to Eurisko by scanning Wilczek's license plate.

66 Scully finds herself in deadly peril because of what booby trap?

67 How do Mulder and Scully kill the COS computer?

68 Who says, "They can do anything they want."

"Ice"

69 Who says, "We're not who we are."

70 How do the two Arctic expedition members die during the transmission of the video message?

71 Mulder and Scully add four members to their expedition team. Name two of them.

72 What does the expedition team find on the body of the tranquilized dog?
  A. Black nodules
  B. Radioactive fleas
  C. A slimy mud

73 TRUE OR FALSE: Three other bodies are found. It is determined they died of strangulation.

74 Two things are found in Richter's blood. What are they?

75 They discover that the wormlike organism enters the brain, resulting in what from the host?

76 Who is accused of killing Dr. Hodge?
  A. Mulder
  B. Scully
  C. Da Silva

77 What happens when a worm is dropped into Da Silva's ear?

78 Mulder's attempts to return to the ice station for further investigation of the incident are stopped when what happens?

79 Who tells Mulder, "They're your people."

"Space"

80 What happened to Col. Marcus Belt when he was an astronaut?

81 How much time is left when the space shuttle launch is aborted?

82 Who turns out to be the anonymous letter writer?
   A. Communications Commander Michelle Generoo
   B. Former astronaut Avery Reynolds
   C. Col. Marcus Belt

83 TRUE OR FALSE: X rays show that an auxiliary power unit has been tampered with.

84 What causes Generoo to crash on the way back to Mission Center?

85 Two hours and eighteen minutes into the shuttle flight, the Space Center loses communication. As a result, what can't they do?

86 Who says, "There's someone outside the ship."

87 What is written on Belt's desk blotter?
   A. "Help me."
   B. "They're coming for me."
   C. "Scully is one of them."

88 What do Mulder and Scully see in Belt's face?

89 What is the name of the shuttle's alternative landing site?

90 What do doctors ultimately determine about Belt's condition?

"Fallen Angel"

91 What are the circumstances of Deputy Sheriff Wright's death?

92 Where does the unidentified object crash and what is its speed?

93 TRUE OR FALSE: The name of the UFO mop-up group is called Operation Bang Tango.

94 Who gives Mulder the unofficial go-ahead to investigate the fallen object site?

95 What is the name of the UFO conspiracy theorist Mulder encounters?
  A. Max Von Braun
  B. David Renfro
  C. Max Fenig

96 We discover that Mulder has been writing magazine articles under a pseudonym. What is it?

97 What did Sheriff Wright and the three firefighters die of?

98 What does Mulder notice while helping Fenig recover from an epileptic seizure?

99 A UFO hovers over the town of Townsend. What happens to Fenig?

100 Who says, "He's gone. They got to him first."

101 During a hearing, Mulder is told what about Fenig?

A. He was a double agent who had now been reassigned.
B. His body had been discovered in a cargo container.
C. He was the byproduct of a human-alien mating.

102 Who says, "Mulder active is less dangerous than having him exposed to the wrong people."

"Eve"

103 What is the name of the disease that kills Joel Simmons?

104 Mulder examines the body and determines what about the wounds and blood removal?

105 Who tells Mulder and Scully about "the men from the clouds"?
A. Teena
B. Deep Throat
C. Agent Rodriguez

106 What do Mulder and Scully discover about Cindy?

107 Where did the in-vitro fertilization take place?

108 Why was Dr. Sally Kendrick fired from her post at the Stapes Center?

109 What is the signal to go meet with Deep Throat?

110 TRUE OR FALSE: The code names for the U.S. eugenics experimental subjects were Adam and Eve.

111 Which are the only remaining Eves prone to suicide?

112 How many chromosomes does each Eve have?

113 What happens when the Eves reach age twenty?
A. They die.

B. They develop homicidal tendencies.

C. Their aging process speeds up.

114 TRUE OR FALSE: Eves 9 and 10 are accidentally burned to death.

115 Which Eve is still on the loose?

"Fire"

116 Mulder does what for the first time in the episode "Fire?"

117 Phoebe Green, an old flame of Mulder's, holds what job?

118 Where did Mulder and Phoebe have sex?

119 What does Mulder suggest is the cause of the mysterious burnings of Parliament members?

120 What is the caretaker's name?

A. Edward Baines

B. Bob

C. Francis Devlin

121 TRUE OR FALSE: Mulder has a phobia about fire.

122 What is Bob's true identity?

123 When and how did L'lvely die?

124 Mulder finds Phoebe in a romantic embrace with whom?

125 How is Bob finally captured?

126 Despite suffering fifth- and sixth-degree burns and a 109° temperature, Bob is recovering. Why?

"Beyond the Sea"

127 What were the last words Scully heard from her father before he died?

128 What does Mulder say to Scully for the first time?

129 Death-row criminal Luther Lee Boggs claims what power?

130 Where did the blue cloth Mulder used to trick Boggs come from?
   A. His New York Knicks t-shirt
   B. A shower curtain
   C. A blanket from an adjoining cell

131 What does Boggs call Scully as she is about to leave his cell?

132 What does Boggs warn Mulder to avoid?

133 Boggs channels what memory of Scully's?

134 Who says, "Don't follow Henry to the Devil."
   A. Boggs
   B. Mulder
   C. Deep Throat

135 Who does Boggs claim he will channel at the moment of his execution?

"Genderbender"

136 Actor Nicholas (Krycek) Lea made his first appearance in *The X-Files* in the episode "Genderbender" as what character?

137 What happens to the woman after her sex partner dies?

138 What is the cause of the series of mysterious deaths?

139 What is the name of the group linked to the murders?
A. The White Light
B. The Kindred
C. The Children

140 Whose handshake leaves Scully breathless?

141 Who begins choking at the dinner table?

142 What does Mulder recall about the faces at the dinner table?

143 Who says "The Kindred are different."

144 Whom does Scully believe the killer to be?
A. The surviving Eve from the "Eve" episode
B. A transvestite
C. Brother Aaron

145 Name the hotel where Mulder and Scully find the killer.

146 What do the agents find when they invade the Kindred compound?

"Lazarus"

147 What is the connection between Scully and Jack Willis?

148 What does Willis do before he leaves the hospital?

149 TRUE OR FALSE: Willis left his fingerprints on the handle of a scalpel.

150 Where is Willis when Dupre's tattoo materializes on his body?

151 What does Mulder believe has happened to Willis?

152 What is odd about Willis's birthday card to Scully?
   A. Her birthday isn't for another two months
   B. It is printed rather than written
   C. He signs only his last name

153 Who admits to setting Dupre up?

154 What does Mulder hear in the background on the tape of Scully's cel phone?

155 Who says "There's nothing to be afraid of."
   A. Mulder
   B. Scully
   C. Willis

156 How does Willis die?

157 What is inscribed on the watch retrieved from Willis's personal effects?

"Young at Heart"

158 What significance does John Barnett hold in Mulder's life?

159 What does the note found on Mulder's car say?

160 What is listed as Barnett's cause of death?
   A. Heart attack
   B. Gunshot wound to the stomach
   C. Natural causes

161 What does the note found on Purdue's body say?

162 Why was Ridley's medical license revoked in 1979?

163 TRUE OR FALSE: Ridley was doing unauthorized experimentation on children with a disease called progeria.

164 Barnett's aging process has been reversed through the introduction of what into his body?

165 Barnett disguises himself as what to sneak into the recital hall to stalk Scully?
A. An FBI agent
B. A musician
C. A piano tuner

166 How does Mulder kill Barnett?

167 Who attempts to speak to Barnett before he dies?
A. Mulder
B. Scully
C. Cigarette Smoking Man

"E.B.E."

168 In what country is the UFO shot down?

169 What does Scully say the UFO sightings can be attributed to?

170 Name the three Lone Gunmen.

171 How is Scully being monitored by the government?

172 What does Deep Throat give Mulder?

173 Who says "The truth is out there, but so are lies."

174 What do the initials E.B.E. stand for?

175 What does Deep Throat confess to Mulder?
A. He is one of three people who has actually killed an alien.
B. He has secretly funneled information to Mulder through The Lone Gunmen.

C. He is Mulder's father.

176 Who says "The truth will be known."

"Miracle Man"

177 In "Miracle Man" we discover that the first X-File was initiated by whom?

178 What does Samuel do at the fire?

179 Name Hartley's ministry.

180 What is the ministry's slogan?
   A. Believe and you shall live.
   B. Prayer and open arms
   C. Come as you are . . . Leave as you always wanted to be.

181 What happens in the courtroom the day of the bail hearing?

182 What is Mulder's theory about Samuel's powers?

183 How does Samuel die?
   A. He is beaten to death by two thugs.
   B. He hangs himself in his jail cell.
   C. He slashes his body to match Christ's crucifixion wounds.

184 How does Vance die?

"Shapes"

185 The dead Joe Goodensnake belonged to what tribe?

186 What does Mulder discover shortly after being called in to investigate the murder?

187 What is unusual about Joe Goodensnake's body?

188 Who initiated the first X-File and in what year?

189 TRUE OR FALSE: The attacks appear to be occurring in eight-year cycles.

190 What evidence is found after Jim Parker's murder?
  A. Animal tracks
  B. A tuft of fur and another piece of shed skin
  C. Indian headband feathers

191 Name the creature credited with starting the cycle of creature-related attacks.

192 How did Richard Watkins pass on the curse?

193 Who kills Lyle Parker?
  A. Mulder
  B. Scully
  C. Sheriff Tskany

"Darkness Falls"

194 What covers and kills the loggers?

195 The first reports of killings in the area occurred in what year?

196 What happens to the truck on the way to the logging camp?
  A. It is attacked by fireflies.
  B. It gets two flat tires.
  C. It runs out of gas.

197 Mulder and Scully find a cocoon—what do they discover inside it?

198 What released the radiation that caused the mutations of the amoebas?

199 What is Mulder's theory about the insects?

200 At the end of the episode, where are Mulder and Scully found?

"Tooms"

201 Who speaks for the first time in the episode "Tooms"?

202 In this episode, whom does Scully meet for the first time?

203 The judge dismisses Mulder's mutation theory, citing what?
   A. A physical that showed no abnormalities
   B. Tooms does not look one hundred years old
   C. Mulder's erratic past performance with the FBI

204 What did the skeletal remains discovered by Scully and Briggs turn out to be?

205 How does Tooms get into the house of his next intended victim?

206 How does Tooms get to Mulder's apartment?

207 What does Tooms accuse Mulder of?
   A. Bugging his room
   B. Beating him
   C. Following him

208 How is Tooms killed?

"Born Again"

209 How does Detective Rudy Barbala die?

210 Which of the following is true about Michelle Bishop?
 A. She never smiles.
 B. She sees and hears invisible things.
 C. She is adept at origami.

211 TRUE OR FALSE: Michelle likes to dismember and disfigure her dolls.

212 What was the condition of Charlie Morris's body when it was found?

213 What is the name of the gang suspected in Morris's death?
 A. The Black Dragon
 B. Woo Shing Wu
 C. The Yakuza

214 Leon Felder dies in what unusual manner?

215 What does Mulder tell Scully he's discovered about Michelle?

216 Michelle, under regression hypnotherapy, indicates she is twenty-four years old and suddenly screams what?

217 What was the last thing Morris saw before he died?

218 Who begs Michelle to stop trying to kill her husband?

219 Michelle is finally charged with what crime?
 A. No crime
 B. First-degree murder with special circumstances
 C. Second-degree murder and obstructing justice

"Roland"

220 How does Dr. Surnow die?

221 What is the name of the top-secret project the murdered scientists were working on?

222 How did Dr. Grable die?
   A. He was sucked into a jet engine.
   B. He had an auto accident.
   C. He was stabbed.

223 What is Roland the janitor described as being?

224 How does Roland kill Dr. Keats?

225 Dr. Grable's preserved head is in what facility?

226 What does the birth certificate Scully finds indicate?
   A. Roland and Dr. Grable are brothers.
   B. Roland and Dr. Grable are half-brothers.
   C. Roland and Dr. Grable, despite their similar appearance, are not related.

227 Mulder believes that Dr. Grable is not dead but rather . . .

228 Who says "You took my work!"

229 TRUE OR FALSE: Roland is charged with first-degree murder.

230 What is the final temperature reading on the capsule holding Dr. Grable's head?

"The Erlenmeyer Flask"

231 The saying in the opening credits is changed for the first time from "The Truth Is Out There" to what?

232 What kind of trail does the fugitive leave as he jumps into the harbor?

233 To whom does Mulder trace the stolen car?
  A. Dr. Terrence Allen Berube
  B. Ardis Police Captain Roy Lacerio
  C. Inspector Walter Skinner

234 Who tells Mulder "Trust me. You've never been closer."

235 Who is the mystery man who crawls out of the harbor?

236 What does Mulder find at the Emgen Corporation?

237 What happens when the medics try to revive Secare?
  A. He kills them by snapping their spines.
  B. His body releases a gas that disables them.
  C. The medics are knocked out by the Crew Cut Man.

238 Mulder discovers that Dr. Berube has been conducting human experiments with an extraterrestrial virus since what year?

239 TRUE OR FALSE: Deep Throat tells Mulder and Scully that "Roswell was a smokescreen."

240 What is the password Scully uses to get into the High Containment Facility?

241 What does Scully take to trade for Mulder's life?
  A. A vial containing a more advanced bacteria specimen
  B. A list containing the names of Deep Throat's superiors
  C. The body of an alien the size of a human fetus

242 Who kills Deep Throat?

243 Who informs Mulder that the X-Files unit has been shut down?

244 Where does Cigarette Smoking Man hide the alien?
   A. In the basement of his apartment building
   B. In the Pentagon basement
   C. He returns it to the High Containment Facility

2

SEASON TWO

"Little Green Men"

245 What are Mulder and Scully doing now that the X-Files unit has been disbanded?

246 The downturned photo of Mulder's sister Samantha is a signal to do what?
  A. Meet Scully in the parking complex of the Watergate Hotel
  B. Contact Skinner at his office
  C. A very "X-Files" kind of case has just surfaced

247 What game is Mulder playing with Samantha the night she's abducted by aliens?

248 What is the name of the top-secret government UFO team authorized to use terminal force?

249 What password does Scully use to break into Mulder's computer?

250 What does Scully say when confronted by another agent staking out Mulder's apartment?

"The Host"

251 Which writer was pressed into service as the monster in the episode "The Host"?
  A. Howard Gordon

William B. Davis as the Cigarette Smoking Man. © 1996 Fox
Broadcasting Company. Photo Credit: Ken Staniforth/FOX.

    B. Darin Morgan
    C. Glen Morgan

252 Where does the dead Russian's half-eaten body wash up?

253 What does Scully find while performing an autopsy on
the dead Russian?

254 Who tells Mulder he has a friend at the FBI?

255 Where is the Flukeman seen for the first time?

256 How does the Flukeman escape after killing the marshal?
  A. It slithers down a campsite toilet.
  B. It finds an outlet back into the sewer system.
  C. It crawls into a nearby lake.

257 What news does Scully call Mulder with?

258 It is determined that the creature originally came on a ship hauling salvage from where?

"Blood"

259 What is Ed Funsch's occupation when he receives the "Kill 'em all" message?

260 What did Taber do after receiving his "Kill 'em all." message?
  A. He killed his boss.
  B. He killed four strangers before being killed by a security guard.
  C. He killed his wife.

261 What clue does Taber's autopsy produce?

262 How does Mrs. McRoberts kill the mechanic?

263 What appliance directs Mrs. McRoberts to kill Mulder?

264 Scully's autopsy on Mrs. McRoberts reveals what?

265 What do Scully and Mulder figure out about Funsch?

266 Where is Funsch's first sniper assault?

267 What is the message on Mulder's cel phone?

"Sleepless"

268 Where is the body of Dr. Saul Grissom found?
  A. On the Tri-Boro Bridge

B. Inside his apartment
C. On the steps outside FBI headquarters

269 Name Mulder's partner on this case.

270 How did Grissom actually die?

271 What vision does Willig see when he dies?

272 What is the name of the renegade Special Forces and Recon squad?

273 How long has it been since Cole has slept?
A. Twenty-four years
B. Seventeen years
C. Fourteen years

274 What does Mulder tell Scully about Cole after the SWAT shootout?

275 TRUE OR FALSE: The name of the Long Island cafe is the Hell Hole.

276 Dr. Francis Girardi is the innovator of what radical surgery?

277 How is Girardi shot?

278 Who kills Cole?

279 Who says, "Every problem has a solution."
A. Alex Krycek
B. Mr. X
C. Cigarette Smoking Man

"Duane Barry"

280 What is Mulder doing when he's located by Krycek?

281 During the hostage negotiations, Krycek is sent on what errand?

282 Why is Mulder sent to the hostage scene?

283 TRUE OR FALSE: Mulder gets into the travel agency where Barry is holding the hostages by impersonating a hostage negotiator.

284 Scully discovers what about Duane Barry's mental state?

285 What does Duane Barry reveal to Mulder?

286 What do X rays of Duane Barry's body reveal?

287 What does the the metal in Barry's sinus and gums contain?
  A. Small radio transmitters
  B. Etched markings
  C. Microscopic vials of green fluid

288 Barry comes to in the hospital to visions of what?

289 Whom does Duane Barry kidnap?

"Ascension"

290 To whom does Mulder speak at the scene of Scully's kidnapping?

291 Who believes that Mulder's too close to the case?
  A. Krycek
  B. Assistant Director Skinner
  C. Cigarette Smoking Man

292 What does the dead cop's police car video show?

293 What is the name of the mountain where the tram is discovered?

294 What does Mulder find in the trunk of Scully's car?

295 Who is accused of killing Duane Barry?
  A. Mulder
  B. Scully
  C. Krycek

296 Who says, "Killing Mulder risks turning one man's religion into a crusade."

297 Who says, "They have something on everyone, Mr. Mulder."

298 Mulder notices what in Krycek's car?

299 What does Skinner take it upon himself to do?
  A. He puts a contract on Krycek.
  B. He reopens the X-Files.
  C. He warns Cigarette Smoking Man to stay away from the investigation.

"3"

300 What is Mulder flipping through while he is alone in his office?

301 What is written on the victim's wall in human blood?

302 Name the blood bank and the mystery employee.
  A. American Red Cross; David
  B. The Hollywood Blood Bank; Frank
  C. Main Street Blood Bank; Rebecca

303 How does the Son die?

304 What is the burning disease called?

305 Where does Mulder meet Kristen?
  A. The Hamlet Lodge

B. Club Tepes

C. The bus terminal

306 What does Mulder find in the oven in Kristen's house?

307 How does the Unholy Spirit die?

308 Who kills Kristen?

309 What do firefighters find in the ruins of Kristen's house?

A. Four piles of charred bones

B. A stack of human skulls bathed in blood

C. Four piles of ashes and bones

"One Breath"

310 The episode "One Breath" featured the use of this signal for the first time.

311 What does Scully's tombstone say?

312 What are the instructions in Scully's living will?

313 What does Frohike notice about Scully's charts?

A. Her DNA level is dangerously low.

B. Her DNA level is dangerously high.

C. Abnormal protein chains in her blood.

314 Name the newest Lone Gunman.

315 Whom does Mulder accuse of being responsible for what happened to Scully?

A. Cigarette Smoking Man

B. Krycek

C. Agent Randel

316 What kind of cigarettes are left in the machine?

317 Who says, "I've watched presidents die."

318 What does Mulder hand Scully after she regains consciousness?

"Firewalker"

319 What is the name of the volcanic exploration robot?

320 Pierce left the project six weeks before the mysterious deaths began after an argument with whom?

321 What does Mulder find while going over Trepkos's notes?

322 What does Jesse tell Scully about Trepkos?

323 TRUE OR FALSE: A spore bursts out of Tanaka's throat.

324 What does the autopsy on Tanaka's body indicate?

325 Who kills Ludwig, and how?

326 Who says, "The earth holds some truths best left buried."
    A. Mulder
    B. Trepkos
    C. Scully

327 Why did Trepkos destroy his notes and kill Pierce?

"Red Museum"

328 What phrase is written on Gary Kane's back?

329 What is the vegetarian cult called?

330 Which of these famous people is found to be a "Walk-in"?
    A. Abraham Lincoln
    B. Adolf Hitler

C. Mikhail Gorbachev

331 Name the restaurant where Mulder and Scully eat.

332 How is Dr. Jerrold Larson killed?

333 Whom does Scully recognize Crew-Cut Man as?

334 Who kills Crew-Cut Man?

"Excelsius Dei"

335 Nurse Charters is raped by . . .

336 The prime suspect is . . .
   A. Andrew Frieberg, who looks amazingly like an older Mulder
   B. Hal Arden
   C. Stan Phillips

337 What had Dr. Grago been treating Hal Arden with at the time of his death?

338 Who ignores Gung's warning and takes too many pills?

339 How does attendant Tiernan die?

340 Dorothy sees what ghostly apparition surrounding Scully?

341 TRUE OR FALSE: Mulder finds a mushroom farm in the basement of the old age home.

342 What power does Gung claim the mushrooms have?

343 Who is locked in the bathroom, which is rapidly filling with water?
   A. Mulder and Nurse Charters
   B. Scully and Gung
   C. Stan and Dorothy

344 What happens after Dr. Grago gives a shot of atropine to Stan?

"Aubrey"

345 Name the motel where Detective Morrow meets Lieutenant Tillman.

346 Whose remains are discovered in the field?

347 TRUE OR FALSE: The razor cuts on Cheney's remains spell the word "sister."

348 Morrow says what about the most recent crime victim?
   A. Her last name is Cheney.
   B. The woman was pregnant at the time of her murder.
   C. The woman is somebody she has seen in a recurring dream.

349 The suspect, Harry Cokely, was convicted of what crime in 1945?

350 Scully suggests that Morrow has cryptomnesia. What is cryptomnesia?

351 What condition is Morrow in when she awakens from a nightmare?

352 What does Linda Thibedeaux admit to Mulder and Scully?
   A. She became pregnant by Cokely but had a miscarriage.
   B. She became pregnant by Cokely but had an abortion.
   C. She became pregnant by Cokely but gave the child up for adoption.

353 Whose remains are found beneath Morrow's floorboards?

354 What happens when Morrow attacks Mrs. Thibedeaux?

355 Who has petitioned to adopt Morrow's still-unborn child?
  A. Mrs. Thibedeaux
  B. Lieutenant Tillman
  C. Cokely's younger sister

"Irresistible"

356 What did Donnie Pfaster do to the corpse of Jennifer?

357 Agent Bock attributes the mutilations to aliens. Mulder believes they are the work of
  A. Aliens
  B. An escalating fetishist
  C. A local group of Satan worshipers

358 What is the main focus of Scully's field report?

359 What does Pfaster request of the streetwalker he brings back to his apartment?

360 The prostitute's body is found in a muddy field. What body parts are missing?

361 What is Scully's dream?

362 Where does Agent Busch find a fingerprint?

363 TRUE OR FALSE: A raid on Pfaster's home produces a refrigerated finger.

364 While bound and gagged in a closet, what does Scully imagine Pfaster as?

365 What does Scully do after being rescued?

"Die Hand Die Verletzt"

366 Who calls for a prayer to the Lord of Darkness?

367 TRUE OR FALSE: Jerry's penis and eyes were removed from his body.

368 Who was the last person to check out the book *Witch Hunt: A History of the Occult In America?*
  A. Dave
  B. Jerry
  C. Jim Ausbury

369 What rains down from the sky?

370 We discover that the body of Jerry was displayed in accordance with what ritual?

371 The drinking fountain draining counter-clockwise is consistent with what condition?
  A. The Coriolis Effect
  B. The Northern Ridge Factor
  C. Northern Hemisphere Shunt

372 Shannon claims she has had three babies. Where are the bodies buried?

373 What disease did the regular science teacher contract?

374 What does Paddock steal from Scully?

375 When Mulder and Scully return to the basement where they handcuffed Ausbury, what do they find?

376 Who saves Mulder and Scully by shooting Paul and Deborah?
  A. Phyllis Paddock
  B. Pete Calcagni

C. Shannon

377 What final message is written on the chalkboard?

"Fresh Bones"

378 What is the first horrible vision John McAlpin has before his death?

379 Where are the Haitians being held?

380 What does Mulder buy from Chester Bonaparte?

381 When McAlpin's morgue slab is pulled out, what do we see?
  A. McAlpin's badly decomposed body
  B. The body of a dog
  C. Frogs

382 There are traces of the substance tetrodotoxin in McAlpin's body. What is tetrodoxin?

383 Who says, "Fresh bones. They pay good."

384 What threat did Bauvais make to Colonel Wharton?

385 Mulder and Scully chase Chester around a corner. What do they find?
  A. A cat
  B. A raven
  C. A snake

386 How does Scully cut her hand?

387 What vision does Scully have in the car?

388 Mulder falls to the ground when Wharton does what?

389 What is Wharton's final fate?

"Colony"

390 These three characters make their first appearance in the episode "Colony."

391 What comes out of Dr. Prince's body when he is stabbed?

392 What does Mulder receive by way of his e-mail?

393 Who left the last message on the classified ad voice mail?

394 After killing Baker, the Pilot morphs into . . .

395 Ambrose Chapel informs Mulder and Scully that the clones were created by the Russians under what code name?
   A. Gregor
   B. Operation Multiplicity
   C. Duplicates

396 Following the Dickens chase, what does Scully notice under her shoe?

397 Who says, "I changed it to 'Trust Everyone.' "

398 Who does the woman at Mulder's parents' home claim to be?

399 What does Scully find at the warehouse?

400 Name the motel where Scully is hiding out.

401 Why doesn't Scully get Mulder's cell-phone call?

"End Game"

402 What would kill the Pilot?

403 What do we learn about alien blood?
   A. Human exposure to it is fatal.

B. It causes extreme mutation in humans.
C. It destroys all red blood cells.

404 Why do the alien clones work in abortion clinics?

405 Where does the Scully-for-Samantha trade take place?

406 Where does Samantha's letter tell Mulder to meet her?

407 Who says, "We knew you could be manipulated."

408 What does Mulder's e-mail to Scully say?

409 Who gets into a fight with Mr. X in Mulder's apartment building?
   A. Skinner
   B. The Pilot
   C. Blevins

410 Who is the sole survivor on the USS *Allegiance*?

411 What does the Pilot tell Mulder during their final confrontation?

412 Scully convinces doctors that Mulder is suffering from what?

"Fearful Symmetry"

413 What does the trucker discover in the middle of the road?

414 TRUE OR FALSE: It is determined that the elephant died of exhaustion.

415 What is the name of the anti-animal-captivity group?
   A. Roam Free
   B. Wild Again Organization
   C. Live Free

416 What is the town of Fairfield known for?

417 What kills the WAO assistant?

418 Sophie the gorilla begins signing what words?

419 Who kills the tiger?

420 What is Mulder's theory regarding Sophie?

421 How is Lang killed?

422 Who is locked in the room with Sophie?
A. Mulder
B. Scully
C. Ambrose

423 Sophie signs what message to Mulder before disappearing into the beam of light?

424 What does Mulder's concluding voiceover suggest?

"Død Kalm"

425 Name the lone member of the USS *Ardent* to not abandon ship.

426 What does Mulder theorize the ship disappearances are the result of?
A. UFO abductions
B. Aberrant ocean currents
C. Wormholes

427 TRUE OR FALSE: On the trip to the *Ardent*, Scully gets seasick.

428 Mulder, Scully, and Trondheim begin to age rapidly. What does Scully suspect the cause is?

429 Where does the only drinkable water come from?

430 What do blood and urine tests show?

    A. High levels of carbon
    B. High levels of salt
    C. A mutated form of fungal organism

431 Why does Mulder not respond to the recycled water treatment?

432 TRUE OR FALSE: Trondheim drowns when the ship's hull bursts into the sewage hold.

433 How is Mulder's sickness treated?

"Humbug"

434 What did Scully put in her mouth?

435 The murdered Alligator Man had what skin condition?

436 What is unusual about the pastor eulogizing the Alligator Man?
    A. He has no arms.
    B. He has no legs.
    C. He is missing one arm and one leg.

437 Who drives a metal stake into his son's chest?

438 Mr. Nutt has a degree in what subject?

439 What does Dr. Blockhead do while being interviewed by Mulder and Scully?

440 Name the freak who will eat anything.

441 Who has Jim-Jim the Dog-Faced Boy grown up to become?

442 TRUE OR FALSE: Sheriff Hamilton is caught burying a potato in his yard.

443 After escaping the Tabernacle of Terror, whom does Leonard attack?

    A. Dr. Blockhead

    B. The Conundrum

    C. Scully

444 What did Lanny die of?

445 Who said, "It's probably something I ate."

"The Calusari"

446 How does Teddy die?

447 Who said "You marry a devil. You have a devil child."

448 Scully speculates that Golda has . . .

    A. The Demeter Effect

    B. Munchausen's-By-Proxy syndrome

    C. Devil's Lesions

449 How does Steve die?

450 What pecks and claws Golda to death?

451 Who tells Mulder "The evil here has existed throughout history under many names."

    A. Calusari Elder

    B. Maggie

    C. Karen

452 What do we discover about Charlie's birth?

453 What manifestation takes place during the final hospital ritual?

454 What is the warning given Mulder by the Calusari Elder?

"F. Emasculata"

455 In what country is Dr. Torrence infected by a disease?
A. Kenya
B. Costa Rica
C. Brazil

456 What does the package to Bobby Torrence contain?

457 What disease is the prison's deadly outbreak initially attributed to?

458 TRUE OR FALSE: A pustule explodes in Scully's face when she opens the body bag.

459 Which convict is dead and which is missing?

460 What do the pustules contain?

461 TRUE OR FALSE: Scully is infected by a parasite.

462 How is Paul finally killed?

463 How is the parasite–Pinck Pharmaceutical conspiracy covered up?

464 Who said, "I stand right on the line you keep crossing."
A. Scully
B. Cigarette Smoking Man
C. Skinner

"Soft Light"

465 Chester kills Newirth in what manner?

466 What is Kelly Ryan's relationship to Scully?
A. She's Scully's cousin.
B. She's one of Scully's former academy students.
C. She is Scully's former partner.

467 What does Mulder think the killings are the result of?

468 Where does Chester evaporate the two police officers?

469 How did Chester develop the shadow-killing alter ego?

470 What does Chester describe his shadow as?

471 TRUE OR FALSE: Chester believes the government wants to perform a brain-suck on him.

472 An attempt by Mr. X and two associates to kidnap Chester fails when . . .
  A. A blackout ends and the lights go back on.
  B. Chester is not in his hospital room.
  C. The shadow killer emerges and kills the two agents.

473 Who kills Dr. Davey?

474 Who said "I never made any promises and I didn't kill Chester."

"Our Town"

475 The late George Kearns held what job?

476 TRUE OR FALSE: Kearns sued the government over stress-related headaches.

477 What happens to Paula after Sheriff Arens shoots her?

478 Kearns and Paula experienced symptoms similar to each others'. What were they?

479 What does the mystery disease turn out to be?
  A. Redfield's dementia
  B. Creutzfeldt-Jacob disease
  C. Brazarra flu

480 What is discovered when the lake is dragged?

481 Scully thinks the killings are the work of a cult. What does Mulder think?

482 In what year was the picture of Chaco and the natives taken?

483 What does Mulder find in the cabinet?

484 How is Chaco killed?

485 Mulder shoots the masked man. Who is he?

"Anasazi"

486 Who said, "The earth has a secret it needs to tell."

487 What alias does computer hacker Kenneth Soona use?
A. The Thinker
B. The Mole
C. Mack the Knife

488 What does Soona's digital audiotape contain?

489 Scully recognizes that the tape code is written in what language?
A. Iranian
B. Navajo
C. Sumerian

490 Who does Cigarette Smoking Man pay a surprise visit to?

491 What happen to Scully when she returns to Mulder's apartment?

492 Who kills William Mulder?
A. Cigarette Smoking Man
B. Krycek
C. The Stealth Man

493 Who shoots Mulder?

494 What does Scully discover once the tape is translated?

495 What does "Anasazi" mean?

496 Who calls Mulder on his cel phone?

497 What kind of container is Mulder trapped in?

498 Who said, "Burn it!"

3

SEASON THREE

"The Blessing Way"

499 Who was introduced as Cigarette Smoking Man's boss in the episode "The Blessing Way"?

500 Who said, "Something lives only as long as the last person who remembers it."
   A. Mulder
   B. Albert Hosteen
   C. Cigarette Smoking Man

501 TRUE OR FALSE: Scully finds Muller's body at the wreckage of the boxcar.

502 What do the men in the mysterious helicopter steal from Scully?

503 What does Scully discover when she returns to Mulder's desk?

504 Where is the badly injured Mulder discovered?

505 What is the name of the healing ceremony performed on Mulder?
   A. The Night of Ten Eagles
   B. The Blessing Way Chant
   C. The Washtahay

Mitch Pileggi as Skinner. © 1996 TWENTIETH CENTURY FOX FILM
CORPORATION.

506 Who appeared in Mulder's dream vision and told him,
"You're the memory, Fox."

507 What does the FBI metal detector reveal about Scully?

508 What message does Scully receive at Mulder's father's
funeral service?

509 Who takes Scully to Mulder's apartment?

510 Who kills Scully's sister Melissa?
  A. Krycek
  B. Wilson
  C. Mr. X

511 Who has the missing digital tape?

"Paper Clip"

512 Who is Victor Klemper?

513 TRUE OR FALSE: Operation Paper Clip is the code phrase for alien experimentation.

514 Who prays over Melissa?
  A. Mulder
  B. Skinner
  C. Albert Hosteen

515 What do Mulder and Scully find at the West Virginia mining site?

516 How do Mulder and Scully escape the mysterious armed men?

517 What does Skinner want to trade the tape for?

518 Who attacks Skinner in the hospital stairwell?

519 How was genetic material unknowingly gathered from U.S. citizens?

520 Who said, "Even in his grave, I hate him still."

521 How many Navajo know the contents of the digital tape?

522 Who said, "I've heard the truth. Now what I want are the answers."

A. Mulder
B. Scully
C. Skinner

"D.P.O."

523 How many people have died in Connerville in the past year?

524 What is unusual about the lightning deaths?
A. All were killed at night
B. All were young men
C. All were fathers

525 Who does Darin have the hots for?

526 What happens to Mulder's cel phone?

527 What do Mulder and Scully discover at the fried-cow site?

528 What do the agents find in Darin's room?

529 What does Darin's hospital chart reveal about him?

530 How is Darin subdued?
A. He steps in a puddle and is electrocuted.
B. He is struck by lightning and knocked unconscious.
C. Mulder shoots him.

"Clyde Bruckman's Final Repose"

531 Who played Stupendous Yappi in "Clyde Bruckman's Final Repose"?

532 Name the TV psychic.

533 What is Clyde Bruckman's occupation?

534 Name the event that caused Bruckman to become obsessed with how people die.

535 What undignified death does Bruckman discuss with Mulder?

536 Who does Bruckman predict Scully will end up in bed with?
  A. Mulder
  B. Bruckman
  C. Skinner

537 Who turns out to be the serial killer?

538 How is the serial killer subdued?

539 How does Clyde Bruckman kill himself?

"The List"

540 Who said, "Fry him."

541 What crawls across Neech's stained pillow?

542 What is the name of the con on Neech's death list?
  A. Speranza
  B. Roque
  C. Johnson

543 TRUE OR FALSE: The guard's head is found in a paint can.

544 Where does the guard's headless body end up?

545 What does Roque tell the Warden about the list?

546 Who is spotted kissing Danielle?
  A. The warden
  B. Parmelly
  C. Speranza

547 Who does Scully believe is responsible for the killings?

548 Who kills Parmelly?

549 How does the warden die?

"2SHY"

550 What is the connection between the four women's mysterious disappearances?

551 What is the name of Virgil Incanto's next online attachment?

552 What is the name of the chat room where Incanto finds his victims?
   A. Love On Line
   B. Heaven
   C. Big and Beautiful

553 What does Scully find on Lauren's body?

554 When Ellen stands Virgil up at the restaurant, who does he attack instead?
   A. A prostitute
   B. A waitress
   C. A woman sitting alone at a nearby table

555 Who describes the killer as "some kind of fat-sucking vampire"?

556 What does Detective Cross notice while questioning Virgil?

557 Who finds Cross's corpse in the bathtub?

558 What alerts Virgil to the fact that the FBI is on to him?

559 Who shoots Virgil?

A. Ellen
B. Jesse
C. Scully

560 It is discovered that how many women are missing in how many states?

"The Walk"

561 What does Lt. Colonel Stans do on his fourth suicide attempt?

562 TRUE OR FALSE: Stans says an apparition that looked like a soldier killed his family.

563 The threat the ghostly voice issues to General Callahan is:
A. "Your time has come, killer."
B. "Kiss your wife and kid goodbye."
C. "Watch your back."

564 How is Captain Draper killed?

565 Who does the FBI mistakenly arrest for the murders?

566 How does the general's son die?

567 Who said, "I'm just the mailman."

568 What does Mulder believe Rappo is capable of?

569 Who smothers Rappo with a pillow?

570 In what cemetary is Rappo denied burial?

"Oubliette"

571 What is Lucy Householder's occupation?

572 Who said, "That's spooky."
A. Mulder

    B. Scully
    C. Lucy

573 How long was Lucy missing?

574 Where has Carl Wade hidden Amy?

575 TRUE OR FALSE: Mulder theorizes that Lucy can see what Amy sees.

576 Why does Scully want to arrest Lucy?

577 What does Mulder believe the bond between Lucy and Amy to be?

578 Where is Lucy land after she escapes?

579 What is Wade doing to Amy as the agents close in?

580 Who shoots Wade?

581 Lucy sacrifices her life for Amy. How does she die?

"Nisei"

582 When do we see the dead alien for the first time?

583 What does Scully say about Mulder's tape?

584 TRUE OR FALSE: The name of the UFO organization whose member list Mulder finds in the satchel is United Watching the Skies.

585 Who kills the Japanese diplomat?
    A. Skinner
    B. The Red-Haired Man
    C. Cigarette Smoking Man

586 What is significant about the women in the UFO group?

587 What does Mulder see when he looks through the warehouse window?

588 Who said, "Monsters begetting monsters."

589 Name the secret medical group performing human-alien experiments.

590 What does Mulder see happening in the train yard?

591 What does Mulder lose while leaping onto the train?
   A. His gun
   B. His cel phone
   C. His identification

"731"

592 Name the site where the deformed creatures are being held.

593 Who said, "There are limits to my knowledge."
   A. Skinner
   B. Mr. X
   C. Cigarette Smoking Man

594 Pendrell tells Scully what about the chip found in her neck?

595 TRUE OR FALSE: Cigarette Smoking Man kills Dr. Zama.

596 Who saves Mulder from being strangled by the Red-Haired Man?

597 The deformed creatures are not alien in origin. What are they?

598 How much time is left when Mulder finally discovers the bomb?
   A. Thirty minutes

B. Forty-eight minutes

C. A little over one hundred minutes

599 What disease does the creature on the train have?

600 Who kills the Red-Haired Man and saves Mulder?

601 Who said, "Apology has become policy."

A. Mulder

B. Scully

C. Skinner

"Revelations"

602 How many stigmatics have been killed over a three-year period?

A. Seven

B. Nineteen

C. Eleven

603 Who said, "He's bleeding again, isn't he?"

604 What is Owen Jarvis doing just before he kidnaps Kevin Kryder?

605 TRUE OR FALSE: Owen tells Kevin that he is his guardian angel.

606 How is Owen Jarvis killed?

607 What does Scully call people whose bodies don't decompose normally?

608 Who is the stigmatic killer?

A. Ronald Hightower

B. Simon Gates

C. Sharon

609 Where has Gates taken Kevin?

610 How does Gates die?

"War of the Coprophages"

611 Name the first scientist to die.

612 Who said, "Scully, what are you wearing?"
A. Mulder
B. The Stoner
C. Skinner

613 How does the teen drug-user kill himself?

614 The medical examiner is found dead, sitting on the toilet. How does Scully theorize he died?

615 What is Bambi's occupation?

616 Who said, "Her name is Bambi?"
A. Sheriff Frass
B. Scully
C. The possessed store clerk

617 Name the wheelchair-bound scientist.

618 Over what item does a fight breaks out in the grocery store?

619 What does Mulder say to the roach?

620 With what does Mulder squash the roach?

"Syzygy"

621 Who said, "Maybe if we weren't virgins, we wouldn't be so scared."

622 Name the town where the strange doings are going on.
A. Miller's Grove

B. Comity

C. Harmonyville

623 What happens to Boom's coffin at the church service?

624 TRUE OR FALSE: The burn mark on the latest victim's chest resembles a pentagram.

625 How is Eric killed?

626 Name the missing Lhasa Apso.

A. Mr. Tippy

B. Dribbles

C. Ratso

627 What does the Ouija board spell?

628 What does Scully see when she enters Mulder's room?

629 Terri and Margi were both born on what day?

630 How is Scott killed?

631 What is Mulder's final comment to Scully as they speed out of town?

A. "Shut up and drive."

B. "Sure. Fine. Whatever."

C. "I guess your feet weren't too small."

"Grotesque"

632 Who is the first victim of the serial killer?

A. A male model

B. A cop

C. An undercover FBI agent

633 Who gets bitten during the John Mostow arrest?

634 TRUE OR FALSE: John Mostow is suspected of killing seven men in South America.

635 What is Bill Patterson's relationship to Mulder?

636 What does Mulder find in Mostow's secret room?

637 Who told Mulder he was insane?

638 What does Scully find in Mulder's apartment?
  A. A bloody knife
  B. Pictures of gargoyles
  C. Autopsy pictures of the murder victims

639 Where is Mulder attacked by the serial killer?

640 Whose fingerprints does Scully find on the knife blade?
  A. Mulder's
  B. Patterson's
  C. Nemhauser's

641 Who turns out to be the new serial killer?

"Piper Maru"

642 What does the French diver see?

643 TRUE OR FALSE: Melissa's murder investigation has become inactive after five months.

644 Name the ship reported to have salvaged a UFO from the ocean floor.
  A. Talapus
  B. Neptune
  C. Deep Six

645 The alien life form lives in what substance?

646 The ship's video shows the sunken ship and what object?

647 Name Scully's old family friend.

648 To whom does Mulder handcuff himself while in Hong Kong?

649 By whom was Mulder's prisoner killed?
  A. Cigarette Smoking Man
  B. Alex Krycek
  C. Zeus Faber

650 Krycek said the digital tape was hidden where?

651 What possessed person takes over Krycek's body in the rest room?

"Apocrypha"

652 To whom does the hospitalized crewman tell his secrets?

653 Who gave the okay to have the bodies of Mulder's attackers destroyed?
  A. Mulder
  B. Cigarette Smoking Man
  C. Well-Manicured Man

654 TRUE OR FALSE: DNA reports indicate that the man who shot Skinner also shot Scully's sister.

655 Mulder theorizes that the oily substance is used by the alien creature to do what?

656 Who goes to the ice rink locker to retrieve the tape?

657 Where does Mulder meet the Well-Manicured Man?
  A. Central Park
  B. The Watergate Hotel Bar
  C. Well-Manicured Man's office

658 TRUE OR FALSE: The UFO downed during World War II is called a Foo Fighter.

659 The black substance jumps from Krycek to where?
A. Into a UFO
B. Onto Cigarette Smoking Man
C. Onto an unidentified government agent

660 Where is Krycek trapped?

"Pusher"

661 What creature appears on the cover of the *Weekly World Informed* in the episode "Pusher"?

662 Where is Pusher arrested by the FBI?

663 Name the agent who meets with Mulder and Scully.
A. Adam Riley
B. Frank Burst
C. Davidson

664 What is the Japanese word Mulder spots on a police car?

665 TRUE OR FALSE: Pusher induces an agent to shoot at Mulder and Scully at the golf course.

666 Modell once applied to join what organization?

667 How is Skinner subdued?

668 What do Mulder and Scully find in Modell's refrigerator?

669 How does Modell kill Agent Burst?

670 What information does a computer monitor show about Modell?

671 Modell forces Mulder to play what game?

"Teso Dos Bichos"

672 What is the name of the ancient tribe whose remains are unearthed in Ecuador?

673 What kills Roosevelt?

674 Who said the researcher was killed for working on the project?
A. Mona
B. Dr. Lewton
C. Mulder

675 Whom does Scully see as the prime suspect in the murders?

676 TRUE OR FALSE: Scully finds a dead cat in Dr. Lewton's engine.

677 What is the yellow liquid Bilac drinks called?
A. Bolak
B. Yaje
C. Spruce

678 What climbs out of the toilets?

679 How does Bilac escape?

680 What attacks Mulder and Scully in the tunnels?

681 What does the official report on the deaths state?

"Hell Money"

682 What do the Chinese characters found inside the crematory oven mean?

683 Hell Money is used to pay off spirits during what holiday?

684 What does Scully find on the body of the man discovered in the shallow grave?

A. Chinese characters
B. Surgical scars
C. A pentagram tattoo

685 Who said, "I'm just as white as you are."
A. Hsin
B. Detective Chao
C. Mr. X

686 TRUE OR FALSE: Mulder and Scully discover that the game is being conducted in a Chinese restaurant.

687 Chao discovers what about the game?

688 Who shoots the doctor?

689 How does Chao die?

"Jose Chung's From Outer Space"

690 Name the teens abducted by aliens.

691 Who said, "Truth is as subjective as reality."
A. Scully
B. Mulder
C. Jose Chung

692 Who said to Mulder, "You really bleeped up this case."

693 What does Harold remember the alien doing?

694 TRUE OR FALSE: The large alien is called Lord Kinbote.

695 Name two people who have seen the Men in Black.

696 What does Mulder do when he sees the alien corpse?
A. He steps gingerly around it.
B. He yelps.
C. He runs to find Scully.

697 Who hosts the Dead Alien video?

698 What game show host helps Mulder deal with the man in black?

699 Who said "How the hell should I know?"
  A. Jose Chung
  B. Mulder
  C. Lord Kinbote

700 Name the agents in Jose Chung's book.

"Avatar"

701 Where does Skinner meet the prostitute?
  A. In a hotel bar
  B. In the lobby of FBI Headquarters
  C. At a party for Agent Rogers

702 What is Skinner's recurring dream?

703 Scully notices what about the dead prostitute's body?

704 What is Skinner's wife's name?

705 How long have Skinner and his wife been separated?

706 Scully discovers that Skinner is being treated for what affliction?

707 Mulder theorizes that Skinner's dream woman is what creature?
  A. An Opy
  B. A Succubus
  C. Regent's Avenger

708 How is the madam killed?

709 Name the killer who is stopped by Skinner.

A. David Branford
B. Alexis French
C. His identity remains unknown

710 Skinner reaches into his desk drawer and does what?

"Quagmire"

711 What object is Dr. Bailey retrieving when he's attacked by the monster?

712 What is Scully's dog named?

713 What is the name of the sea serpent?
A. Big Blue
B. Nessie Too
C. Farraday

714 The fisherman hooks the body of what victim?

715 TRUE OR FALSE: The bait shop owner is leaving fake dinosaur tracks in the woods when he's attacked by the monster.

716 Where do Mulder and Scully end up when their boat is sunk by the monster?

717 Mulder theorizes that the increase in attacks is due to what?
A. The depletion of the frog supply
B. The rising of the water temperature
C. The creature being in heat

718 Mulder kills the monster. What does it turn out to be?

"Wetwired"

719 Where do we see the body of the first murder victim?

A. In a hole
B. In the kitchen
C. In a car trunk

720 What is the occupation of a second person who also went on a murder spree in the same neighborhood?

721 What does Scully see outside her hotel room?

722 TRUE OR FALSE: A woman shoots her next-door neighbor after seeing her husband having sex with another woman.

723 What does Mulder tell Skinner that he thinks Scully is suffering from?
A. Drug-induced dementia
B. Paranoid psychosis
C. Flashbacks to her abduction

724 Why was Mulder immune to the mind-control device?

725 Scully pulls a gun on Mulder at whose house?

726 Who kills Dr. Stroman and the cable guy?

"Talitha Cumi"

727 What is the name of the fast-food restaurant featured in this episode?

728 Who does Cigarette Smoking Man meet?

729 What word does Mrs. Mulder write on a note pad?
A. Retro
B. Palm
C. Alien

730 TRUE OR FALSE: Jeremiah Smith is captured in the FBI building.

731 Where does Mulder find the alien stiletto?

732 Jeremiah Smith morphed into two people. Who are they?

733 We discover that Cigarette Smoking Man is dying of what disease?

    A. AIDS

    B. Lung cancer

    C. Spinal Polegra

734 Mulder said, "Do you want to smoke this?" before doing what to Cigarette Smoking Man?

735 What docs Mr. X say to Mulder after they fight?

    A. "You're a dead man."

    B. "Scully is doomed."

    C. "Don't turn around."

736 TRUE OR FALSE: Mulder pulls his gun as the bounty hunter charges him.

4

Season Four

"Herrenvolk"

737 This cinematographer was fired halfway through the production of "Herrenvolk."
A. John S. Bartley
B. Ron Stannet
C. Jon Joffin

738 What UN operative makes her first appearance in "Herrenvolk"?

739 How is the telephone-line repairman killed?

740 TRUE OR FALSE: Scully stabs the bounty hunter in the back.

741 How many Jeremiah Smiths are working for the Social Security Administration?

742 Whom do the girl clones look like?

743 Who responded to Scully's X signal?

744 What did Mulder do to avoid the deadly bee stings?

745 Who told Mulder, "He tells you nothing of the whole."

746 What does a dying Mr. X write in his own blood?

747 Who cures Mulder's mother?

"Home"

748 What item is used to deliver the Peacocks' mutant baby?
A. A knife
B. A fork
C. A spoon

749 Name the Peacocks' home town.

750 Name the town's sheriff and deputy.

751 TRUE OR FALSE: The mutant baby's cause of death was being buried alive.

752 What song was playing on the Peacocks' car radio.

753 How is the sheriff killed?

754 Mulder theorizes that the father of the mutant baby is whom?
A. The sheriff
B. All three Peacock brothers
C. The deputy

755 What is the headline on the newspaper Mulder finds in the Peacock house?

756 Where do they find Mrs. Peacock?

757 Scully theorizes that Edmund Peacock is what?
A. The son of the sheriff
B. The half brother of the deputy
C. The father and brother of the other two Peacock brothers

758 Which Peacock brother survives?

"Teliko"

759 Where is the murdered airline passenger found?

760 Who said, "This investigation should begin and end under a microscope."
A Skinner
B. Dr. Brewin
C. Scully

761 Mulder said, "Scully's got a date . . . with a dead man" to whom?

762 What kind of plant is the mystery seed taken from Owen Sanders' body from?

763 Aboah pulls what out of his mouth?

764 TRUE OR FALSE: Mulder finds Aboah hiding in a drainpipe.

765 What are the Teliko?

766 TRUE OR FALSE: Aboah's X ray shows that a third of his brain is missing.

767 Who gets hit by a seed in the condemned building?

768 How does Scully finally stop Aboah?

"Unruhe"

769 Why does Mary stop at the store?

770 TRUE OR FALSE: The developed Polaroid photo is a distorted picture of Mary screaming.

771 Mulder clicks off Polaroid shots with the lens covered and sees what on the developed pictures?
A. Mary screaming with ghostly figures around her
B. Ghostly figures surrounding a bloody knife
C. Mary's dead boyfriend

772 Name the drug Mary has been given.

773 How was Mary given a lobotomy?

774 Another woman is abducted by a man speaking what language?
 A. French
 B. German
 C. Chinese

775 What does the word "Unruhe" mean?
 A. Undead
 B. Unrest
 C. Man Insane

776 What are Schnauz's demons called?

777 Mulder develops another picture that shows what?

778 In what language does Scully speak to Schnauz?

"The Field Where I Died"

779 Name the cult central to this episode.

780 Who made the mysterious call to the FBI?

781 TRUE OR FALSE: The leader of the cult is named Freddy.

782 Mulder believes the cult leader is using which part of the Bible to control his followers?
 A. Genesis
 B. Leviticus
 C. Revelations

783 Melissa begins to speak in whose voice?

784 Melissa tells Mulder that she saw what?

785 Who does the picture of Civil War soldier Sullivan Biddle look like?

786 How do the cult members commit mass suicide?

"Sanguinarium"

787 Who scrubs his fingers until they bleed?

788 TRUE OR FALSE: Mulder believes the patient murder is the result of psychotic dementia.

789 The burn marks on the floor of the operating room are in what shape?

790 What did nurse Waite put on the body of the skin peel patient?

791 What did Mulder say after seeing the broom on the porch?

792 TRUE OR FALSE: Nurse Waite vomits up straight pins.

793 Where does the word Roodmass appear?
   A. On the operating room wall
   B. On Nurse Waite's calendar
   C. On Dr. Franklin's office door

794 Name three dates of the Witch's Sabbath.

795 Who said, "Vanity. All is vanity."
   A. Scully
   B. Mulder
   C. Dr. Shannon

796 What is Dr. Jack Franklin's true identity?

797 What does Mulder find on the operating room floor?

"Musings of a Cigarette Smoking Man"

798 Which Lone Gunman was marked for death in "Musings of a Cigarette Smoking Man" before Carter changed the ending?
   A. Byers

B. Frohike

C. Langley

799 What phrase is on Cigarette Smoking Man's cigarette lighter?

800 Cigarette Smoking Man's mother died of what disease?

801 What were Mulder's first words after being born?
A. "JFK"
B. "Subvert"
C. "Abduction"

802 Cigarette Smoking Man was directly responsible for the death of . . .
A. John F. Kennedy
B. Martin Luther King
C. Robert F. Kennedy

803 Where was Cigarette Smoking Man when he smoked his first cigarette?

804 TRUE OR FALSE: Cigarette Smoking Man's nom de plum is Raul Bloodworth.

805 Cigarette Smoking Man may have been responsible for . . .
A. Moving the Rodney King trial to Simi Valley
B. Fixing the Oscars
C. Keeping the Buffalo Bills from winning the Super Bowl

806 Who said, "You'll never believe what we got for Christmas."

807 Who murders the alien?

808 Name the the publisher that finally accepts Cigarette Smoking Man's manuscript.

809 Cigarette Smoking Man said "I can kill him whenever I please . . . but not today." Whom is he talking about?

"Paper Hearts"

810 The red light in Mulder's dream turns into what word?

811 The light turns into what shape on the dead girl's body?

812 How many nights has Mulder had the dream?
   A. Every night for a week
   B. Three nights
   C. Every night for a month

813 What are the name and former occupation of the suspected killer?

814 Who said "I used to think that missing was worse than dead."

815 How many hearts do they find in the book *Alice in Wonderland*?

816 TRUE OR FALSE: Mulder dreams that the killer abducted his sister.

817 How is it determined that the fifteenth victim is not Samantha?

818 How does Mulder trick the killer?

819 Where does the killer take his latest victim?

"El Mundo Gira"

820 What color is the rain?

821 Mulder says what in response to Scully's purple rain remark?

The work of a mythical beast on the episode "El Mundo Gira."
© 1996 Fox Broadcasting Company. Photo Credit: Ken
Staniforth/FOX.

822 TRUE OR FALSE: "Chubacabra" means "the demon."

823 Who said "Two men, one woman . . . trouble."
    A. Mulder

B. Scully
C. Skinner

824 What does Scully discover is the cause of Maria's death?

825 Mulder theorizes that the enzyme comes from where?

826 Where is the third fungus victim found?

827 Who is discovered to be spreading the disease?
A. Agent Lozano
B. Eladio Buente
C. The Coyote

828 Fungus on a peanut kills who?

829 What does the old woman see in her version of the final conflict?

830 Where do the brothers go?

"Tungunska"

831 Scully is sworn in in front of what committee?

832 Scully is threatened with being charged with what crime?
A. Contempt of Congress
B. Attempted murder
C. Obstruction of justice

833 Who is the first victim of the oily worms?

834 Who kills the militia truck driver?

835 Who said, "You're an invertebrate scum sucker!"
A. Skinner
B. Mulder
C. Scully

836 What is in the Russian diplomat's pouch?

837 TRUE OR FALSE: Mulder hides Krycek at Skinner's apartment.

838 Krycek swears at Mulder in this language

839 What year did the meteor hit Tungunska?
   A. 1896
   B. 1908
   C. 1943

840 Oily worms are poured on Mulder's body. What part of his body do they enter?

"Terma"

841 What does *e pur si muove* mean?

842 Who is the old Russian's letter from?

843 The prisoners are being tested to find a cure for which disease?
   A. Ryker's Syndrome
   B. Black Cancer
   C. Smallpox

844 TRUE OR FALSE: The woman killed by the old Russian is a virologist.

845 What do the Russians peasants do to Krycek?

846 While in jail, Scully reads up on what subject?
   A. Smallpox
   B. Fungus
   C. Blood clotting

847 Who kills the occupants of the nursing home?

848 Where is the bomb?

849 Where do Mulder and Scully believe the rock comes from?

850 Who is the KGB hitman's new boss?

"Never Again"

851 TRUE OR FALSE: The storyline for "Never Again" was inspired by Gillian Anderson's tattoo.

852 Who was originally set to direct "Never Again" until the Director's Guild said no?

853 Who played the voice of the tattoo?

854 Why is Eddie in court?

855 What is the first word spoken by Eddie's tattoo?

856 Where does Mulder go on his vacation?

857 Who is Eddie's first victim?

858 Who said, "I have everything under control."
A. Scully
B. Mulder
C. Eddie

859 How does Eddie mutilate his tattoo?

860 Scully saw what play on her last date?

861 TRUE OR FALSE: The name of the crummy bar is Hard Eight.

862 What kind of tattoo does Scully get?

863 What does the tattoo say just before Scully kisses Eddie?

864 What does Scully discover about the tattoo dye mix?

865 How does Eddie break the tattoo's control?

"Leonard Betts"

866 How is Leonard Betts killed?

867 Where do Mulder and Scully find Betts's head?

868 Scully starts to autopsy the head when what suddenly happens?

869 What is the bathtub in Betts's apartment filled with?
  A. Blood
  B. Iodine
  C. Water

870 What do further tests on Betts's brain reveal?

871 TRUE OR FALSE: Mulder theorizes that Betts has a positive cancer that allows him to regrow body parts.

872 What is Leonard Betts's alias?

873 Betts is handcuffed to his car. How does he escape?

874 Mulder and Scully come to what conclusion about Betts?
  A. He is eating cancer to live.
  B. He is the result of illegal genetic experimentation.
  C. He only has fourteen hours left to live.

875 What does Betts say to Scully during their final showdown?

876 How does Betts die?

877 What is the first sign that Scully has cancer?

"Memento Mori"

878 Who are the first two people to learn of Scully's cancerous tumor?
   A. Mulder and Skinner
   B. Mulder and Cigarette Smoking Man
   C. Skinner and Cigarette Smoking Man

879 What happens when Scully pulls her gun?

880 What happens to Crawford's body?

881 Who said, "You're going to feel like dying."
   A. Scully's mother
   B. Dr. Scanlon
   C. Frohike

882 What's the computer password?

883 Who does Mulder want to meet?

884 Who said, "You can't ask the truth of a man who trades in lies."

885 What does Crawford turn out to be?

886 What was taken from Scully during her abduction?

887 Who goes to Scully and tells her to stop the cancer treatment?
   A. Byers
   B. Frohike
   C. Skinner

888 What does Mulder say while hugging Scully?

"Kaddish"

889 How was Issac Luria killed?

890 What was the first white supremacist strangled while watching a tape of?

    A. Hiter's speeches

    B. The murder of Issac Luria

    C. Bugs Bunny cartoons

891 Whose fingerprints were found on the victim's body?

892 Who is buried in Issac Luria's grave?

893 TRUE OR FALSE: The book found in the coffin bursts into flame.

894 What name is on the book cover?

895 How is the third white supremacist killed and where is his body found?

896 What is the magic word?

897 What does "golem" mean?

898 Who created the golem?

899 How is the golem destroyed?

"Unrequited"

900 What is on the back of the king of hearts?

901 Name the radical paramilitary group.

902 Who does Markham say is the killer?

903 What does Teager give Gary Davenport's wife?

904 Where is General Steffen killed?

905 Mulder theorizes that Teager has the ability to do what?

906 Who said, "He did it again, didn't he?"

    A. Denny Markham

   B. Scully
   C. Agent Johnson

907 TRUE OR FALSE: Covarrubias tells Mulder the US government wants the generals dead.

908 What does Teager give Danzinger?

909 What are Teager's last words?

"Tempus Fugit"

910 What is the name of the UFO researcher on the doomed flight?

911 What does Mulder get Scully for her birthday?

912 How many minutes are missing?

913 What do the NTSB men do to the body of the assassin?

914 TRUE OR FALSE: The lone survivor of the crash is the drunk.

915 Where is Max's girlfriend abducted from?

916 What does Mulder discover while examining the bodies?

917 Where do the aliens return Max's girlfriend?
   A. The crash site
   B. The air crash examination hanger
   C. The air force control tower

918 What is the name of the lake where Mulder searches for the crashed UFO?

919 What does Mulder find at the bottom of the lake?

"Max"

920 Who said, "He's an FBI agent and he's not going to die."
  - A. Scully
  - B. Mulder
  - C. Skinner

921 Who issues the order to put Mulder under arrest?

922 Mulder has what on his forehead?

923 Where did Sharon meet Max?

924 TRUE OR FALSE: Pendrell dies.

925 Who said, "Oh! Beans and wienies."

926 What caused the airplane and UFO to crash?

927 What is the source of the unexplained radioactivity?

928 Mulder finds the third part of the alien object in which city's airport?
  - A. Syracuse, New York
  - B. Albany, New York
  - C. Los Angeles, California

929 Who sits down next to Mulder?

930 What is Mulder's plane intercepted by?
  - A. A UFO
  - B. An F-15 fighter jet
  - C. A Stealth bomber

"Synchrony"

931 Lucas accuses Jason of what crime?

932 How low has the dead policeman's temperature fallen?
  A. 0°F.
  B. 8°F.
  C. 15°F.

933 Whose fingerprints were found on the dead policeman's body?

934 What does Lisa say when confronted with the two chemical graphs?

935 What happens when Dr. Yonechi is thawed out?

936 Who said "I think the real question is how somebody could have had access to a compound that doesn't exist."
  A. Mulder
  B.. Scully
  C. Lisa

937 The old man stalks Lisa to what building?
  A. The library
  B. Her apartment
  C. The research lab

938 What artifact from the future do Mulder and Scully find in the old man's apartment?

939 Scully once wrote a paper on what subject?

940 We learn that the discovery of time travel has done what to the future?

941 How do the two Jasons perish?

942 The airline ticket on Lisa's desk is to what destination?

"Small Potatoes"

943 What is the tabloid headline?
  A. "Monkey Children Born in West Virginia Town"

B. "Did West Virginia Woman Mate With Visitors From Space?"

C. "Women Monkey Around With Aliens"

944 TRUE OR FALSE: Amanda claims the father of her baby is Luke Skywalker.

945 How many times has Amanda seen *Star Wars*?

946 Who does Mulder discover is the father of the monkey children?

947 Mulder theorizes that the father of the monkey children has what power?

948 How do Mulder and Scully discover that the janitor's father is really the janitor?

949 What does the autopsy of the mummified body indicate?

950 Who said, "I was just here. Where did I go?"
A. The fake Mulder
B. The real Mulder
C. Scully

951 There are two messages on Mulder's answer machine. One is from The Lone Gunmen. Who is the other message from?

952 Who is Marcus?

953 TRUE OR FALSE: Scully and the fake Mulder kiss.

954 How is the janitor kept from morphing?

955 What did Scully say to Mulder as they left the reformatory?

"Zero Sum"

956 What is the occupation of the first bee-sting victim?

957 TRUE OR FALSE: Skinner uses the name Fox Mulder at the forensics lab.

958 Who said "I thought you were part of something called X-Files."
   A. Agent Kautz
   B. Detective Ray Thomas
   C. Skinner

959 Where is Scully throughout this episode?

960 Who said "A man digs a hole, he risks falling into it."
   A. Gray-Haired man
   B. Cigarette Smoking Man
   C. Skinner

961 What model gun is the murder weapon?

962 What killed the entomologist?

963 Name the school where the bees attack.

964 What has been done to Skinner's gun to make it untraceable?

965 TRUE OR FALSE: Skinner fires three shots at Cigarette Smoking Man's head.

966 Who is listening to Marta's conversation with Cigarette Smoking Man?

"Elegy"

967 What is the name of the bowling alley?

968 What words appear after Mulder spills soda on the bowling lane floor?
  A. Death Becomes Her
  B. She Is Me
  C. Goodnight Princess

969 Harold constantly mumbles numbers. What are the numbers?

970 Scully determines that the killer suffers from what compulsive disorder?

971 How does Angie die?

972 What does Scully find in Harold's dresser drawer?

973 Scully shoots the killer who turns out to be whom?
  A. Harold
  B. Nurse Innes
  C. Dr. Alpert

974 Scully realizes she saw the ghost for what reason?

975 Whom does Scully see in her back seat?

"Demons"

976 Who said, "I'm afraid Fox! I'm afraid!"

977 TRUE OR FALSE: The blood on Mulder's shirt is his own.

978 Mulder's car is registered to whom
  A. Officer Allen
  B. David Cassandra
  C. Amy Cassandra

979 In a dream, who tells Mulder "You're a little spy."

980 What is conspicuous about the suicide victims?

981 Name the drug found in Mulder's blood sample.
A. Rygol
B. Ketamine
C. Martika

982 What is the name of the UFO magazine?

983 TRUE OR FALSE: Scully theorizes that all the suicide victims were suffering from Waxman-Geschwind Syndrome.

"Gethsemane"

984 What has the tag line "The Truth Is Out There" been replaced by?

985 What does Scully tell the FBI Inquiry Board that Mulder has become?

986 Where and in what condition is the body of the alien found?

987 What relative does Scully meet at her mother's party?

988 TRUE OR FALSE: The mystery man pushes Scully down a flight of stairs.

989 What is the mystery man's name?
A. Michael Kritschgau
B. David Anderson
C. Dead Eye Man

990 TRUE OR FALSE: The mystery man claims the US government gave Scully cancer.

991 What happens to the body of the alien?

992 Mulder cries as he watches what scientist on television?

993 What first-season character returns to head up the FBI Inquiry Board?

994 It is reported that Mulder is dead. How has he reportedly died?

5

X-Files: **The History**

The genesis of *The X-Files* has been reported in detail. Here's a chance to test your knowledge on the creation of the show and some of the significant events surrounding its first four seasons.

995 The two unsold TV pilots created by Chris Carter prior to *The X-Files* are:
    A. *The Intruder* and *Cameo By Night*
    B. *The Nanny* and *Cameo By Night*
    C. *Midnight Caller* and *The Streets*

996 Carter said that *X-Files* was influenced by his love for what two TV shows?

997 When did the Fox network give the official go-ahead for *The X-Files*?

998 Gillian Anderson wore what to her first *X-Files* audition?

999 Where did David Duchovny and Gillian Anderson meet for the first time?
    A. Chris Carter's office
    B. The Fox network building
    C. Duchovny's agent's office

1000 Name the studio where *X-Files* is filmed.

Mulder and Scully investigate the deaths in a Jewish community in "Kaddish." © 1997 Fox Broadcasting Company. Photo Credit: Aaron Rapport/FOX.

1001 TRUE OR FALSE: The first episode of *The X-Files* aired in September 1993.

1002 The name of the episode in which Scully appears in her underwear is:
  A. "The X-Files"
  B. "Deep Throat"
  C. "The Host"

1003 In what episode did Mulder and Scully point guns at each other for the first time?

1004 The Lone Gunmen are introduced in what episode?

1005 The abduction of Mulder's sister is shown for the first time in what episode?

1006 Gillian Anderson missed only one episode during her pregnancy. Name the episode.

1007 *X-Files* writers Glen Morgan and James Wong left the show after the second season to develop their own show. Name the show.

1008 Duchovny and Anderson renegotiated their contracts in 1995. How much did each get?

1009 Gillian Anderson's pregnant belly played a bit part in which episode?
  A. "Ascension"
  B. "The Big Drop"
  C. "The Host"

1010 David Duchovny received his first story credit on what episode?

1011 David Duchovny received his second story credit on what episode?

1012 The episode title "Piper Maru" came from what source?

1013 Gillian Anderson's allergic reaction to cats surfaced in what episode?

1014 The first meeting between Mr. X and Cigarette Smoking Man took place in what episode?

1015 TRUE OR FALSE: Glen Morgan and James Wong returned to *The X-Files* on the condition that actors in their former series *Space: Above And Beyond* get parts in their episodes.

6

WHAT'S YOUR FOX MULDER I.Q.?

1016 Fox Mulder was born . . .
   A. April 14, 1960
   B. October 13, 1961
   C. October 17, 1961

1017 What was Mulder's place of birth?

1018 What was his father's name?

1019 What is his mother's name?

1020 What is his sister's name?

1021 TRUE OR FALSE: Mulder's sister was abducted by aliens on November 27, 1973.

1022 Mulder went to what college and majored in what subject?

1023 What nickname did Mulder receive while at the FBI Academy?
   A. Straight A
   B. Dr. Strange
   C. Spooky

1024 What was the subject of his memorable academy paper?

Agent Mulder is trapped in a Russian gulag where he learns of alien/human hybrid experiments being performed on prisoners. © 1996 FOX BROADCASTING COMPANY. PHOTO CREDIT: KEN STANIFORTH/FOX.

1025 How old was Mulder when he joined the FBI?

1026 Before heading up the X-Files, Mulder served in these two FBI branches.

1027 TRUE OR FALSE: Mulder wears glasses.

1029 Mulder likes what?
  A. Pornography
  B. Soccer
  C. Guns

1029 What is Mulder's address?

1030 Mulder's office is in:
  A. The basement
  B. Next to Director Skinner's office
  C. Next to the men's room

7

WHAT'S YOUR DANA
SCULLY I.Q.?

1031 What is Scully's full name?

1032 What is her date of birth?
A. February 23, 1964
B. April 19, 1963
C. August 12, 1963

1033 TRUE OR FALSE: Scully's birthplace is unknown.

1034 What was her father's name and occupation?

1035 What is her mother's name and occupation?

1036 Name Scully's three siblings.

1037 Name two cities in which Scully spent her childhood.

1038 Scully spent one year at what California university?

1039 What did she major in?

1040 She transferred to which university and received what degree?

1041 What was the title of her senior thesis?

1042 After college, Scully went to work for the FBI in what capacity?

Mulder and Scully.

1043 Early in her FBI career Scully had a relationship with what agent?

1044 TRUE OR FALSE: Scully was assigned to the X-Files in 1993.

8

WHAT'S YOUR DAVID DUCHOVNY I.Q.?

1045 Name the date and year David Duchovny was born.

1046 What are his mother's and father's names?

1047 Name Duchovny's older brother and younger sister.

1048 Duchovny went to which well-known prep school?
A. Wiggins
B. Collegiate
C. Kennedy

1049 Duchovny had two different nicknames. What were they?

1050 He received a degree in which subject at what university?

1051 He went on to earn a masters degree in what subject at which university?

1052 TRUE OR FALSE: Duchovny began taking acting lessons at the famous New York Actors Studio.

1053 His first paying acting role was in what?
A. *Friday the 13th, Part IV*
B. A Lowenbrau beer commercial
C. An episode of *Cheers*

David Duchovny as Agent Fox Mulder. PHOTO CREDIT: MICHAEL GRECCO/FOX.

1054 What was Duchovny's first movie role?

1055 Duchovny had a small role in what Harrison Ford film?

1056 He played a bar customer in what Rob Lowe-James Spader movie?

1057 If you blinked you missed Duchovny in this low budget erotic thriller. What was it?

1058 Duchovny appeared in what film starring a member of *Married . . . With Children*?

1059 TRUE OR FALSE: He starred opposite Mimi Rogers in the movie *Killing Ground*.

1060 He played which cross-dressing DEA agent on *Twin Peaks*?

1061 Duchovny used to read his poetry regularly at what Los Angeles club?

1062 What role did Duchovny play in the movie *Ruby*?

1063 Duchovny's appearance in this cable movie turned into a regular host slot when it spun off into a series. Name it.

1064 What part did Duchovny play in the movie *Chaplin*?

1065 He played opposite Brad Pitt in which NC-17 rated movie?

    A. *Baby Snatcher*
    B. *Kalifornia*
    C. *Venice/Venice*

1066 Name the two former girlfriends of Duchovny's who have appeared in *X-Files* episodes.

1067 What is Duchovny's dog's name?

    A. Blue

   B. Chaos
   C. Bad Dog

1068 Duchovny has been linked romantically to . . .
   A. Winona Ryder
   B. Lisa Loeb
   C. Rosalind Chao

1069 TRUE OR FALSE: Duchovny guest-starred as a gay man on *The Larry Sanders Show*.

1070 Name the movie in which Duchovny plays a mob doctor.

1071 Duchovny appeared on *Celebrity Jeopardy* opposite these panelists.

9

WHAT'S YOUR GILLIAN ANDERSON I.Q.?

1072 Name the date and place where Gillian Anderson was born.

1073 What are her parents' names?

1074 What are the names of Anderson's younger brother and sister?

1075 After years in London, the Anderson family relocated to which US city?
    A. Grand Rapids, Michigan
    B. Reynolds, Illinois
    C. Detroit, Michigan

1076 TRUE OR FALSE: Anderson attended City High School.

1077 Anderson's first appearance in front of a camera was in a student film. What was its title?

1078 Which of these college theater productions did Anderson appear in?
    A. *A Flea in Her Ear*
    B. *Romeo and Juliet*
    C. *In a Northern Landscape*

Agent Scully faces contempt charges before a United States Senate subcommittee where she deliberately conceals the whereabouts of Agent Mulder. © 1996 Fox Broadcasting Company. Photo Credit: Ken Staniforth/FOX.

1079 Anderson's second appearance in front of a camera was in this experimental film.

1080 Anderson's only job in New York other than acting was in this restaurant.

1081 TRUE OR FALSE: Anderson's big break came in the play *Absent Friends*.

1082 Anderson's first role in a feature-length movie was in what picture?

1083 Anderson fell in love with her costar during the run of which play?

1084 Anderson read what book on tape in order to pay the rent?

1085 Anderson's only TV appearance prior to *The X-Files* was a guest shot on what series?
A. *Beverly Hills 90210*
B. *Class Of '96*
C. *Homicide*

1086 Clyde Klotz, Anderson's former husband, does what for a living?

1087 When were Anderson and Klotz married?

1088 She won what best acting award in 1995?

1089 TRUE OR FALSE: Anderson gave birth to a baby girl on September 25, 1994.

1090 Anderson has done two cartoon voiceovers. One was for *The Simpsons*. Name the other.

1091 Name the TV disaster documentary Anderson narrated.

1092 She was the voice of Eve the Computer in this CD-ROM game.

1093 Anderson made her TV-movie debut in . . .
A. *Dark November*
B. *Hellcab*
C. *Right or Wrong*

10

NUMBERS GAME

Either you never venture too far from your VCR or you have a big brain for numbers if you can answer these exercises in obscura that center around things like addresses, license plate numbers, and other numerical jumbles that zip through each *X-Files* episode.

1094 What is the number on the box in which Cigarette Smoking Man stores the metal object?

1095 What is the license plate number of Mulder and Scully's car in "Deep Throat"?

1096 What is Scully's apartment building number in "Squeeze"?

1097 What is the morgue file number in "The Jersey Devil"?

1098 Mulder and Scully are treated to lunch in "Ghost In The Machine." How much was the bill?

1099 TRUE OR FALSE: Eve 6's IQ is 278.

1100 Mulder and Scully's rental car license plate number in Genderbender is:
    A. 402-J7A
    B. 905-34Y
    C. 889-Y4L

1101 What is Fiore's badge number in "Born Again"?

1102 What is the number on Mulder's basketball shirt in "Little Green Men"?

1103 What is the Marshal's van number in "The Host"?

1104 Name the number of confirmed J-7 kills in "Sleepless"?

1105 Scully's supermarket bill in "Duane Barry" totaled . . .
   A. $9.47
   B. $11.14
   C. $47.11

1106 How many previous victims were there prior to the events in "3"?

1107 How much did the Firewalker Project cost in "Firewalker"?

1108 What was the number of Mulder's hotel room in "Fresh Bones"?

1109 How old is the elephant in "Fearful Symmetry"?

1110 TRUE OR FALSE: Elizabeth's telephone number in "F. Emasculata" is 555-6936.

1111 In "Anasazi," what number is in the title of the book Soona is reading?

1112 What is Scully's apartment number in "The Blessing Way"?

ANSWERS

Season One

1 The following story is inspired by actual documented accounts.

2 "Nobody down here but the FBI's least wanted."

3 Ethan Minette, a Congressional lobbyist

4 A

5 TRUE

6 The letter X; he didn't know why.

7 C

8 Kidnapping her husband

9 B

10 TRUE

11 Reporter

12 The Yellow Base

13 A

14 That is where Roswell UFO crash wreckage is stored.

15 Paul Mossinger

16 On a running track

17 B

18 His liver was ripped out.

19 The FBI's Violent Crimes Division

20 A

21 1903

22 He's an Animal Control officer.

23 66 Exeter Street

24 103

25 Scully's apartment

26 He has an abnormal muscle and skeletal system and a rapidly declining metabolic rate.

27 A

28 Lake Okobogee

29 B

30 The Center for UFO Studies

31 TRUE

32 B

33 Holtzman

34 They are classified fragments of defense department satellite transmissions.

35 The sand at the site has turned to glass.

36 A white wolf

37 Darlene, Ruby's mother

38 B

39 1947

40 A nudie magazine

41 A

42 Roger Crockett

43 Her godson's birthday party

44 The police shoot her.

45 She has given birth.

46 Cirque du Soleil

47 C

48 A military contractor

49 A desk plaque slides across a desktop.

50 Their throats were crushed from the inside.

51 B

52 Robert Dorlund

53 He is shoved away by an unseen force

54 Mohammed Malachi; Isfahan

55 FALSE

56 Her bathtub is filled with bloody water.

57 Graves's ghost cuts through the wall where the evidence is hidden.

58 He is electrocuted.

59 Violent Crimes

60 Fourth

61 C

62 The COS computer connects with Scully's computer and retrieves Scully's field notes.

63 He is stuck in an elevator that plunges down from the thirtieth floor.

64 An artificial intelligence adaptive network

65 TRUE

66 An industrial fan that is sucking Scully toward its deadly blades

67 They introduce a viral disc.

68 Deep Throat

69 Captain John Richter

70 They shoot each other in the head.

71 Dr. Denny Murphy, Dr. Nancy Da Silva, Dr. Hodge, Bear

72 A

73 TRUE

74 Ammonium hydroxide and a single-celled creature

75 Aggressive behavior

76 A

77 She is cured of the aggressive-behavior disease.

78 The station is burned to the ground.

79 Hodge

80 He was attacked by an alien while on a space walk.

81 T-minus 3 seconds

82 C

83 TRUE

84 She sees a Martian face appear in the fog in front of her.

85 Rotate the shuttle away from the sun

86 One of the shuttle astronauts

87 A

88 The image of a Martian

89 Kirtland Air Force Base

90 He was suffering from severe dementia.

91 He is enveloped by mysterious flashing lights.

92 West of Lake Michigan; over 800 mph

93 FALSE

94 Deep Throat

95 C

96 M. F. Luder

97 They have fifth- and sixth-degree burns over 90 percent of their bodies.

98 He has a V-shaped scar behind his left ear.

99 His ears begin to bleed and he vanishes.

100 Mulder

101 B

102 Deep Throat

103 Hypovolemia

104 They resemble those of alien cattle mutilations.

105 A

106 She looks exactly like Teena.

107 The Luther Stapes Center for Reproductive Medicine

108 She had conducted unauthorized experiments in eugenics.

109 A series of clicks on the telephone

110 TRUE

111 Eves 7 and 8

112 Fifty-six

113 B

114 FALSE

115 Eve 8

116 Kisses a woman

117 She is a Scotland Yard inspector.

118 On Sir Arthur Conan Doyle's tombstone

119 Pyrokinesis

120 B

121 TRUE

122 Cecil L'lvely

123 He died in a satanic cult sacrifice in 1963 and in a London tenement fire in 1971.

124 Sir Malcolm

125 Phoebe splashes accelerant on him and he catches fire.

126 Rapid regeneration of his fundamental basal-cell tissue

127 "Goodnight, Starbuck"

128 He calls her by her first name.

129 He has the ability to channel spirits and demons.

130 A

131 "Starbuck"

132 The white cross

133 The time she snuck a cigarette at age fourteen

134 A

135 Scully's father

136 The disco pick-up

137 She morphs into a man

138 Heart attacks

139 B

140 Brother Andrew's

141 Brother Aaron

142 They were the same faces he saw in the 1930s photos.

143 Brother Andrew

144 B

145 The Hotel Catherine

146 A large, round, flattened imprint in the ground

147 He was an Academy instructor and former boyfriend.

148 He cuts off three of Dupre's fingers to get at his wedding ring.

149 FALSE

150 Dupre's house

151 Dupre has returned to Willis's body.

152 A

153 Lula, Dupre's wife

154 He hears the sound of a plane taking off.

155 C

156 Complications of diabetes

157 Happy 35th, Love D

158 Barnett was Mulder's first case after he joined the FBI.

159 "A hunted Fox eventually dies."

160 A

161 "Funeral for Fox's friends . . . then for Fox."

162 For research malpractice and misuse of a government grant

163 TRUE

164 Reptile regenerative cell morphogens

165 C

166 With a single shot from his service revolver

167 C

168 Iraq

169 Lightning and swamp gas

170 Byers, Langley, and Frohike

171 They inserted a surveillance device inside her pen.

172 A recent photo of a UFO

173 Scully

174 Extraterrestrial Biological Entity

175 A

176 Deep Throat

177 J. Edgar Hoover

178 He brings a dead man back to life.

179 Miracle Ministry

180 C

181 The courtroom is invaded by a swarm of locusts.

182 He is able to manipulate the electromagnetic system in the human body.

183 A

184 Cyanide poisoning

185 The Trego tribe

186 Recently shed skin in the shape of a human hand and wrist

187 He has fangs.

188 J. Edgar Hoover; 1946

189 TRUE

190 B

191 The Manitou

192 Through his son

193 C

194 Something that looks like a swarm of green fireflies

195 1934

196 B

197 The mummified remains of a man

198 The eruption of Mount St. Helens

199 He believes they were hatched from prehistoric insert eggs deposited by Mount St. Helens.

200 Inside a cocoon-filled Jeep

201 Cigarette Smoking Man

202 Assistant Director Walter S. Skinner

203 B

204 A suspected Tooms victim from 1933

205 By squeezing through a barred window

206 By hiding in the trunk of Mulder's car

207 B

208 He is crushed in the machinery of an escalator.

209 He is propelled through a window.

210 A, B, and C

211 TRUE

212 His right eye had been gouged out and his left arm was cut off with a chainsaw.

213 B

214 His scarf becomes tangled in a bus door as it drives away.

215 She was conceived around the time Morris was murdered.

216 "They're killing me!"

217 A plastic deep sea diver

218 Anite Fiore

219 A

220 He is sucked into a jet engine

221 The Icarus Project

222 B

223 An idiot savant

224 He dunks Keats's head into liquid nitrogen and then shatters it.

225 The Avalon Foundation cryogenics department

226 A

227 In a rarefied state of consciousness

228 Arthur Grable, speaking through Roland

229 FALSE

230 150° Fahrenheit

231 "Trust No One."

232 A trail of green blood

233 A

234 Deep Throat

235 Dr. William Secare

236 A flash labled Purity Control

237 B

238 1947

239 TRUE

240 "Purity Control"

241 C

242 The Crew-Cut Man

243 Skinner

244 B

Season Two

245 Mulder is doing electronic surveillance and Scully is teaching.

246 A

248 Stratego

248 The Blue Berets

249 "Trustno1"

250 She is feeding the fish.

251 B

252 The New Jersey sewers

253 A sluglike creature coming out of his liver

254 Mr. X

255 The Newark County sewage processing plant

256 A

257 The fluke creature is attempting to multiply.

258 The Chernobyl disaster area

259 He is a postal worker.

260 B

261 A chemical compound normally found in plants

262 She hits him with a wrench and stabs him with an oil can spout.

263 Her microwave oven

264 Her blood contains adrenaline levels two hundred times above normal.

265 He's phobic about blood.

266 The Franklin Community College blood fair

267 "All done and bye bye"

268 B

269 Alex Krycek

270 He was killed by intense heat without visible external burns.

271 He is gunned down by bloodied Vietnamese.

272 J-7

273 A

274 Cole has the power to produce telepathic imagery.

275 FALSE

276 Brainstem surgery that eliminates the need for sleep

277 By the vision of a J-7 firing squad

278 Krycek

279 C

280 Swimming laps in a pool

281 To get coffee

282 He knows UFO jargon.

283 FALSE

284 A gunshot wound has destroyed the moral center of his brain.

285 The government always cooperates with the aliens.

286 He has pieces of metal in his gums, sinus cavity, and abdomen and drill holes in his left and right rear molars.

287 B

288 White lights and aliens

289 Scully

290 Scully's mother

291 B

292 Scully inside the trunk of her car

293 Skyland Mountain

294 Her gold cross necklace

295 A

296 Cigarette Smoking Man

297 Senator Richard Matheson

298 Cigarette butts from the Cigarette Smoking Man

299 B

300 A swimsuit calendar

301 "John 52:54"

302 B

303 Sunlight burns him to death.

304 Gunther's disease

305 B

306 A blood-filled loaf of bread

307 Kristen impales her on a wooden peg.

308 She kills herself.

309 C

310 The masking-tape X signal

311 Dana Katherine Scully, 1964–1994, Loving Daughter and Friend—The Spirit Is the Truth—John 5:07

312 To stop life support once her Glasgow Outcome Scale reaches a certain level

313 C

314 The Thinker

315 A

316 Morleys

317 Cigarette Smoking Man

318 Her cross

319 Firewalker

320 Volcanologist Daniel Trepkos

321 Trepkos refers to an unknown subterranean organism.

322 He became paranoid after stopping his medication.

323 TRUE

324 His lungs contained sand.

325 Trepkos kills Ludwig with a flare gun.

326 B

327 He wanted to prevent spore contagion

328 "He Is One."

329 The Church of the Red Museum

330 A and C

331 Clay's BBQ

332 He dies in a plane crash.

333 The man who killed Deep Throat

334 Sheriff Mazeroski

335 An invisible entity

336 B

337 An experimental Alzheimers drug called Depranil

338 Stan Phillips

339 An invisible force pushes him through a window.

340 Three old men in bathrobes

341 TRUE

342 They facilitate contact with dead ancestors.

343 A

344 Dorothy says the spirits are gone.

345 Motel Black

346 Agent Sam Cheney

347 FALSE

348 C

349 Rape and attempted murder

350 The power to capture consciously forgotten information

351 She is covered with blood with the word "sister" carved into her chest.

352 C

353 Tim Ledbetter's

354 The word "sister" appears on both of their chests.

355 B

356 He cut off her hair.

357 B

358 Necrophiliacs

359 He asks that she take a bath and shampoo her hair.

360 Some of her fingernails and her fingers

361 Scully dreams that she's performing an autopsy on herself.

362 In the dead streetwalker's nail polish

363 TRUE

364 The alien from a previous dream

365 She breaks down and cries.

366 The Crowley High School PTC

367 FALSE

368 A

369 Toads

370 The Rites of the Azazel

371 A

372 In the basement of her home

373 A flesh-eating bacteria

374 Her pen

375 Digested meat and bones next to a snakeskin

376 B

377 "Goodbye. It's been nice working with you."

378 Maggots in his cereal bowl

379 The Folkstone INS processing center

380 A voodoo charm

381 B

382 It is a poison found in puffer fish.

383 Chester Bonaparte

384 The Marines' souls would be taken one by one.

385 A

386 On a garland of thorns placed around her steering wheel

387 A man rises out of her hand and grabs her by the throat.

388 Plunges a knife into the ground

389 He is buried alive.

390 Mulder's parents and the Bounty Hunter

391 Green blood

392 The obituaries of three abortion doctors

393 Dr. Aaron Baker

394 Agent Barrett Weiss

395 A

396 A spot of green ooze

397 Mulder

398 Mulder's long-lost sister Samantha

399 Four male clones and an alien fetus

400 The Vacation Village Motor Lodge

401 She is in the shower.

402 Piercing the base of his skull

403 A

404 To gain access to human fetal tissue

405 On the Old Memorial Bridge

406 The Women's Health Services Clinic

407 The Samantha clone

408 "Don't follow him and don't risk your life."

409 A

410 Lieutenant Terry Wilmer

411 Samantha is alive.

412 Hyperviscosity Syndrome

413 A dead elephant

414 TRUE

415 B

416 Animal disappearances and UFO activity

417 A tiger

418 "Light. Afraid."

419 Ambrose

420 She is pregnant and afraid of having her baby taken away.

421 An invisible force slams a crate down on him.

422 A

423 "Man. Save. Man."

424 Alien conservationists are involved in saving Earth species.

425 Captain Barclay

426 C

427 FALSE

428 Chemicals with extra electrons that attack DNA proteins

429 The sewage processing system

430 B

431 He's extremely dehydrated from being seasick.

432 TRUE

433 Synthetic hormones

434 A cricket

435 Ichthyosis

436 A

438 Dr. Blockhead

438 Hotel Management

439 He pounds a nail into his nose.

440 The Conundrum

441 Sheriff James Hamilton

442 TRUE

443 B

444 Cirrhosis of the liver

445 The Conundrum

446 He is killed by an amusement-park train ride.

447 Golda

448 B

449 He's choked to death by a garage door opener.

450 Two roosters

451 B

452 He had a twin who died at birth.

453 The walls bleed.

454 "You must be careful. It knows you."

455 B

456 A body part with a pulsating sore

457 A flulike illness

458 FALSE

459 Steve is dead; Paul is missing.

460 The larvae of a parasite-carrying insect

461 FALSE

462 A sniper shoots him.

463 It is blamed on a post office error.

464 C

465 Chester's shadow slips under the hotel room door and evaporates Newirth.

466 B

467 Spontaneous human combustion

468 In a train station

469 He was locked inside a particle generator and received a quantra bombardment.

470 A black hole that splits molecules into component atoms

471 TRUE

472 A and C

473 Mr. X

474 Mr. X

475 Federal Poultry Inspector

476 TRUE

477 She falls into the chicken-feed grinder.

478 Headaches and irritability

479 B

480 Piles of human bones

481 He thinks cannibals did it.

482 1944

483 Shrunken heads

484 He is beheaded by the masked man.

485 Sheriff Arens

486 Albert Hosteen

487 A

488 UFO intelligence files beginning in the 1940s

489 B

490 Mulder's father

491 She is grazed by a bullet fired through the window.

492 B

493 Scully

494 Her name is on it.

495 The ancient aliens

496 Cigarette Smoking Man

497 A railroad refrigerator car

498 Cigarette Smoking Man

Season Three

499 Well-Manicured Man

500 B

501 FALSE

502 A copy of the government alien files

503 The tape copy of the government alien files is gone.

504 Hiding in underground tunnels

505 B

506 Deep Throat

507 A computer chip has been implanted in the base of her neck.

508 She is in danger of being killed by someone she knows.

509 Skinner

510 A

511 Skinner

512 A World War II Nazi scientist

513 FALSE

514 C

515 Cabinets full of medical files

516 Through the mine's secret door

517 He wants Mulder and Scully's safety and their reinstatement into the FBI.

518 Krycek

519 Through smallpox vaccinations

520 Mrs. Mulder

521 Twenty-one

522 B

523 Four

524 B

525 His boss's wife

526 It starts smoking.

527 A shoeprint that has melted into the ground

528 A picture of his boss's wife

529 That he has an electrolyte imbalance

530 B

531 Jaap Broeker

532 Stupendous Yappi

533 Insurance salesman

534 The death of rock star the Big Bopper

535 Autoerotic asphyxiation

536 B

537 The hotel bellhop

538 Scully shoots him.

539 An overdose of pills

540 Warden Brodeur

541 Two flies

542 B

543 TRUE

544 In the warden's chair

545 "You're number five."

546 B

547 Parmelly

548 Danielle

549 Neech attacks him, resulting in a fatal car crash.

550 They all answered a personal ad.

551 Ellen

552 C

553 A digestive enzyme

554 A

555 Scully

556 A bandage on his hand

557 Monica

558 He sees an artist's rendering of his face.

559 A

560 Forty-seven women in five states

561 He throws himself into scalding hot water.

562 TRUE

563 A

564 She is drowned.

565 Roach

566 He's buried under sand.

567 Roach

568 Astral projection

569 Stans

570 Arlington National Cemetery

571 A waitress

572 B

573 Five years

574 In the basement of his house

575 TRUE

576 The blood on her clothes matches Amy's blood.

577 An empathic transference

578 In Carl Wade's basement

579 Dragging her through a river

580 Mulder

581 She drowns.

582 When it is being put into a body bag

583 "This is even hokier than the one they aired on the Fox network."

584 FALSE

585 B

586 They all had implants put in the base of their neck.

587 A UFO

588 Senator Matheson

589 731

590 A living alien is being put on a train.

591 B

592 Hansen's Disease Research Facility

593 B

594 It replicates the brain's memory function.

595 FALSE

596 The train conductor

597 They are lepers.

598 C

599 Hemorrhagic fever

600 Mr. X

601 B

602 C

603 Michael Kryder

604 He is telling ghost stories to children.

605 TRUE

606 He is strangled.

607 Incorruptibles

608 B

609 To a recycling plant

610 He is ground up in a shredding machine.

611 Dr. Bugger

612 A

613 He hacks himself to death with a razor blade.

614 A brain aneurysm

615 USDA government researcher

616 B

617 Dr. Ivanov

618 Bug spray

619 "Greetings from planet earth."

620 An X-file

621 Terri

622 B

623 It begins to burn.

624 FALSE

625 He's crushed by motorized bleachers.

626 A

627 Satan

628 She finds Mulder and Detective White making out.

629 January 12, 1979

630 He's impaled on a garage door spring.

631 B

632 A

633 Agent Nemhauser

634 FALSE

635 Patterson is Mulder's former boss.

636 Sculpted gargoyles with human corpses inside them

637 Bill Patterson

638 B

639 Mostow's apartment

640 A

641 Bill Patterson

642 A man is alive inside the sunken ship.

643 TRUE

644 A

645 Oil

646 A World War II figher plane

647 Major Johansen

648 J. Kallenchuk

649 B

650 In a locker

651 Joan Gauthier

652 Mulder's father and Cigarette Smoking Man

653 B

654 TRUE

655 Jump from body to body

656 The Lone Gunmen

657 A

658 TRUE

659 A

660 In an underground missile silo

661 The Flukeman

662 A grocery store

663 B

664 Ronin

665 FALSE

666 The FBI

667 A woman kicks him and sprays mace in his face.

668 Protein drinks and epilepsy medicine

669 He induces a heart attack.

670 He has a tumor.

671 Russian roulette

672 The Amaru

673 A jaguar

674 B

675 Dr. Alonso Bilac

676 FALSE

677 B

678 Rats

679 Through a vent

680 Cats

681 The deaths were caused by animal attacks.

682 Ghost

683 The Festival of the Hungry Ghosts

684 B

685 B

686 TRUE

687 There are no winning tiles in the vase.

688 Chao

689 He's burned alive in the crematory oven.

690 Harold and Chrissy

691 C

692 Detective Manners

693 Smoking

694 TRUE

695 Roky and Blaine

696 B

697 The Stupendous Yappi

698 *Jeopardy*'s Alex Trebek

699 B

700 Diana Lesky and Reynard Muldrake

701 A

702 An old woman is looming over him.

703 There is a phosphorescent glow around her mouth.

704 Sharon

705 Eight months

706 A sleep disorder

707 B

708 She jumps off a roof.

709 C

710 Pulls out his wedding ring and puts it on

711 A beeper

712 Queequeg

713 A

714 The Boy Scout leader

715 TRUE

716 On a rock

717 A

718 An alligator

719 A, B, and C

720 A babysitter

721 She sees Mulder handing a mysterious tape to Cigarette Smoking Man.

722 TRUE

723 B

724 He is red-green color-blind.

725 Her mother's house

726 Mr. X

727 Brothers K

728 Mulder's mother

729 B

730 FALSE

731 Inside a lamp

732 Deep Throat and Bill Mulder

733 B

734 Sticking a gun in his face

735 A

736 FALSE

Season Four

737 B

738 Marta Covarrubias

739 By a bee sting

740 FALSE

741 Five

742 Mulder's sister, Samantha

743 Mr. X

744 He doused himself with gasoline.

745 The bounty hunter

746 The letters SRSG

747 The bounty hunter

748 B

749 Home

750 Sheriff Andy Taylor and Deputy Barney Paster

751 TRUE

752 "Wonderful" by Johnny Mathis

753 He's beaten to death with clubs.

754 B

755 Elvis Presley Dead At 42

756 Under the bed

757 C

758 Edmund

759 In the bathroom

760 B

761 Agent Pendrell

762 A night blooming passion flower

763 A dagger

764 TRUE

765 Spirits of the air

766 FALSE

767 Mulder

768 She shoots him.

769 To have a passport photo taken

770 TRUE

771 A

772 Twilite

773 An ice pick through the eye sockets

774 B

775 B

776 Howlers

777 Scully screaming

778 German

779 Temple of the Seven Stars

780 Sydney

781 FALSE

782 C

783 Sydney

784 "Saw him die in a field where they were standing"

785 Mulder

786 They drink poisoned wine.

787 Dr. Lloyd

788 FALSE

789 A pentagram

790 Leeches

791 "Probable cause"

792 TRUE

793 B

794 April 30, July 31, October 31

795 B

796 Dr. Clifford Cox

797 Dr. Franklin's face

798 B

799 "Trust No One"

800 Lung cancer

801 A

802 A and B

803 In a movie house

804 TRUE

805 A, B, and C

806 Deep Throat

807 Deep Throat

808 Pivotal Publications

809 Frohike

810 "Follow"

811 A heart

812 B

813 John Lee Roche; vacuum cleaner salesman

814 Frank Sparks

815 Sixteen

816 TRUE

817 The skeleton's collarbone was never broken.

818 He takes him to the wrong house.

819 A bus storage yard

820 Yellow

821 "Great album . . . flawed movie."

822 FALSE

823 B

824 A fungus infection

825 Outer space

826 In a construction site toilet

827 B

828 The grocery clrk

829 Aliens coming out of the hills

830 They head for Mexico.

831 The Senate Select Committee on Intelligence and Terrorism

832 A

833 The customs agent

834 Krycek

835 B

836 A rock

837 TRUE

838 Russian

839 B

840 His nose

841 "And yet it moves."

842 Comrade Artezen

843 B

844 TRUE

845 They amputate his left arm.

846 A

847 The KGB hitman

848 Terma, North Dakota

849 Mars

850 Krycek

851 TRUE

852 Quentin Tarantino

853 Jodie Foster

854 He's getting a divorce

855 "Loser."

856 Graceland

857 Miss Schilling

858 A

859 He sticks a lighted cigarette into it.

860 *Glengarry Glen Ross*

861 TRUE

862 A snake with its tail in its mouth

863 "You kiss her and she's dead."

864 It contains a parasite.

865 He sticks his arm in a furnace.

866 He is decapitated in a car crash.

867 In the hospital's bio-waste facility

868 The head's eyes and mouth open.

869 B

870 Full of cancer

871 TRUE

872 Albert Tanner

873 He rips his thumb off.

874 A

875 "You have something I need."

876 He's electrocuted.

877 A nosebleed

878 A

879 Her nose starts to bleed.

880 It dissolves into a green ooze.

881 B

882 Vegreville

883 Cigarette Smoking Man

884 Skinner

885 A genetic hybrid

886 Some of her ova

887 A

888 "The truth will save you, Scully. The truth will save both of us."

889 He was beaten and shot.

890 B

891 Issac Luria

892 Issac Luria

893 TRUE

894 Jacob Weiss

895 He is found hanged in the attic of a synagogue.

896 Amet

897 Matter without form, body without soul

898 Ariel Weiss

899 The first letter in the word Amet is rubbed off.

900 Blood-crossed swords and a human skull

901 The Right Hand

902 Nathaniel Teager

903 Her husband's dog tags

904 In his office

905 He can erase himself from the visual field.

906 A

907 TRUE

908 A list of POWs still in Vietnam

909 Name, rank, serial number, and date of birth

910 Max Fenig

911 An Apollo 11 keychain

912 Nine

913 They mutilate his face and fingerprints.

914 TRUE

915 A motel

916 All their watches have been stolen.

917 A

918 The Great Sacandago lake

919 A dead alien

920 A

921 The Joint Chiefs of Staff

922 Radiation burns

923 In a mental institution

924 TRUE

925 Mulder

926 An F-15 fighter plane fired on them.

927 Max's hat

928 A

929 The NTSB man

930 A

931 Falsifying research data

932 B

933 Jason's

934 The chemical compound does not exist.

935 He bursts into flames.

936 A

937 A

938 A picture of Jason, Lisa, and Dr. Yonechi

939 Time-travel based on quantum physics

940 It has destroyed all future history.

941 They burst into flames and are incinerated.

942 Zurich

943 B

944 TRUE

945 368 times

946 Eddie Van Brundht

947 He can change his appearance.

948 The father calls Mulder by his name.

949 An anomalous muscle structure

950 B

951 A phone sex service

952 Scully's twelfth-grade boyfriend

953 FALSE

954 He's given muscle relaxants.

955 "You're no loser."

956 Postal worker

957 TRUE

958 B

959 In the hospital

960 B

961 Sig-Sauer P-228

962 Smallpox

963 JFK Elementary School

964 The serial numbers have been filed off.

965 TRUE

966 Mulder

967 Angie's Midnight Bowl

968 B

969 Bowling scores

970 Ego Dystonia

971 A heart attack

972 Pictures of the dead girls

973 B

974 She is dying.

975 Harold's ghost

976 Samantha

977 FALSE

978 B

979 Cigarette Smoking Man

980 They all have holes drilled in their heads.

981 B

982 *Abductee*

983 TRUE

984 Believe the Lie

985 A victim of his own false false hopes and his belief in the biggest of lies

986 Frozen in an ice cave

987 Her brother Bill Scully

988 TRUE

989 A

990 TRUE

991 It is taken by government operatives.

992 Carl Sagan

993 Blevins

994 Suicide

The History

995 B

996 *Kolchak: The Night Stalker* and *The Avengers*

997 August 1992

998 A baggy suit

999 B

1000 North Shores Studios

1001 TRUE

1002 A

1003 "Ice"

1004 "E.B.E."

1005 "Little Green Men"

1006 "3"

1007 *Space: Above And Beyond*

1008 Duchovny: $100,000 per episode; Anderson: $60,000 per episode

1009 A

1010 "Colony"

1011 "Anasazi"

1012 It's Gillian Anderson's daughter's name.

1013 "Teso Dos Bichos"

1014 "Wetwired"

1015 TRUE

What's Your Fox Mulder I.Q.?

1016 B

1017 Chilmark, Massachusetts

1018 William Mulder

1019 She is known only as Mrs. Mulder

1020 Samantha Ann Mulder

1021 TRUE

1022 Oxford University; Psychology

1023 C

1024 Serial killers and the occult

1025 Twenty-eight

1026 Violent Crimes and Behavioral Sciences units

1027 TRUE

1028 A

1029 Street and city unknown, Apartment no. 42

1030 A

What's Your Dana Scully I.Q.?

1031 Dana Katherine Scully

1032 A

1033 TRUE

1034 William Scully, Navy captain

1035 Margaret Scully, housewife

1036 William, Melissa, and Charles

1037 San Diego and Annapolis

1038 Berkeley

1039 Forensic Medicine and Pathology

1040 University of Maryland, BA in Physics

1041 *Einstein's Twin Paradox: A New Interpretation*

1042 FBI Academy teacher

1043 Jack Willis

1044 FALSE

What's Your David Duchovny I.Q.?

1045 August 7, 1960

1046 Margaret and Amram

1047 Daniel and Laurie

1048 B

1049 Duke and Doggie

1050 English Literature at Princeton

1051 English Literature at Yale

1052 TRUE

1053 B

1054 *New Year's Day*

1055 *Working Girl*

1056 *Bad Influence*

1057 *Julia Has Two Lovers*

1058 *Don't Tell Mom the Babysitter's Dead*

1059 FALSE

1060 Dennis Bryson

1061 The Largo Pub

1062 J. D. Tippit

1063 *Red Shoe Diaries*

1064 Rollie Totheroth

1065 B

1066 Maggie Wheeler and Perrey Reeves

1067 A

1068 A and B

1069 TRUE

1070 *Playing God*

1071 Stephen King and Lynn Redgrave

What's Your Gillian Anderson I.Q.?

1072 August 9, 1968; Chicago, Illinois

1073 Edward and Rosemary

1074 Aaron and Zoe

1075 A

1076 TRUE

1077 *Three at Once*

1078 A, B, and C

1079 *A Matter of Choice*

1080 Dojo's

1081 TRUE

1082 *The Turning*

1083 *The Philanthropist*

1084 *Exit to Eden*

1085 B

1086 Production design

1087 New Year's Day 1994

1088 A Golden Globe

1089 TRUE

1090 Reboot

1091 *Why Planes Go Down*

1092 *Hellbender*

1093 B

Numbers Game

1094 100041

1095 8216

1096 1419

1097 2242

1098 $8.50

1099 FALSE

1100 A

1101 247

1102 30

1103 4940

1104 4100

1105 B

1106 6

1107 $20,000,000

1108 7

1109 Twelve years old

1110 TRUE

1111 50

1112 35